DISCARD

UNDERSTANDING
PHILOSOPHY

CONTEMPORARY
THOUGHT

UNDERSTANDING PHILOSOPHY

Ancient and Hellenistic Thought

Medieval and Modern Philosophy

Contemporary Thought

UNDERSTANDING
PHILOSOPHY

CONTEMPORARY
THOUGHT

JOAN A. PRICE

CHELSEA HOUSE
PUBLISHERS
An imprint of Infobase Publishing

To Karin and Jack
for all your love, loyalty, and support.
《C &》

Contemporary Thought

Copyright © 2008 by Infobase Publishing

Chelsea House
An imprint of Infobase Publishing
132 West 31st Street
New York NY 10001

Library of Congress Cataloging-in-Publication Data

Price, Joan A.
Contemporary thought / Joan Price.
    p. cm. — (Understanding philosophy)
Includes bibliographical references (p.   ) and index.
ISBN 978-0-7910-8792-3 (hardcover)
1. Philosophy, Modern. I. Title. II. Series.

B791.P65 2008
190—dc22   2007028465

Series design by Erika K. Arroyo
Cover design by Ben Peterson

Printed in the United States of America

Bang KT 10 9 8 7 6 5 4 3 2 1

This book is printed on acid-free paper.

CONTENTS

1
THE UTILITARIANS
Bentham and Mill

It is better to be a human being dissatisfied
than a pig satisfied; better to be Socrates
dissatisfied than a fool satisfied.
—John Stuart Mill

THE INDUSTRIAL REVOLUTION

The Industrial Revolution was a period of dramatic change in
the technological, social, political, and cultural conditions in
the mid-eighteenth and early-nineteenth centuries. Almost all
phases of daily life were affected by these shifts, including the
philosophical thinking of the times.

The Revolution started in Great Britain because it had the
technological means, government support, and a widespread
trade network to support the growth of industry. Although his-
torians disagree over the exact years that the Industrial Revolution began and ended, most would concur that it occurred
in England between 1750 and 1830, transforming that country
from a rural, agriculture-based economy to a town-centered,
increasingly industrialized economy. Manual labor was largely
replaced by industry and machinery, and by 1850, all western
Europe was more or less industrialized.

The increased use of coal and the coming of steam power
improved iron-making techniques, and the development of

7

metal tools and machines, coupled with a growing network of canals, roads, and railways, saw the effects of the Revolution spread throughout Europe, and eventually, to the world.

Until the Revolution, most of the world's population was rural. By the mid-nineteenth century, however, more than half of the people in the industrialized countries lived in cities. The Revolution produced a new class of working poor forced to live in crowded city tenements clustered around plants and factories. Families often lived in one room, and it was not unusual for four or five children to share a bed. The poor living conditions they endured were the result of the owners' use of cheap building materials, the lack of building codes and sanitation, and the factory owners' tendency to regard laborers as property and not as human beings.

This new class of industrial workers included the men, women, and children laboring in the textile mills, pottery works, mines, and other newly developing industries. Children often entered the factories as young as nine years old and worked 12 hours a day. Wages were low, the workers labored long hours, and working conditions were often dangerous.

In England, the laboring class began the long fight for reform. In 1832, the Reform Bill was passed by Parliament, giving voting power to some of those on the lower social and economic scale. Although the bill represented a major victory for the middle class, working conditions often remained poor, and wealthy factory owners continued to repress their workers. Such repression was unacceptable to the British utilitarian philosophers, such as Jeremy Bentham and John Stuart Mill, who were to be responsible for many social reforms.

The Individual and Society

With the growth of industry and the increase in city population, problems for individual landowners arose. To illustrate this issue, think about your commute to school or your job. The road you drive on may have once been a family farm. When the community decided to build the road, it probably offered to buy the land from the owner at a fair market price. If the farm owners decided not to sell, the community could simply force them to leave and pay the owners the price it determined was reasonable, or the fair market value. We see two principles at work here. The first principle is that individual rights—the landowner's right to fair compensation for his land—should be protected. The second principle is that the good of the majority must have priority over the good of any individual. This principle is the philosophy of the utilitarians: "Happiness for the most people." It is sad that the farm owners lost their house and land, but according to utilitarianism, the good of the majority must take precedence over the good of any individual. The utilitarians' "greatest happiness principle" was born from the Industrial Revolution, and it was first introduced by British philosopher Jeremy Bentham.

JEREMY BENTHAM

Jeremy Bentham's ethics and views on law provided much of the social basis for liberal democracy. In Bentham's philosophy, we see the influence of David Hume, an earlier British philosopher who emphasized our capacity for sympathy. Sympathy, said Hume, is the pleasure we feel when we consider another person's happiness. In utilitarianism, the pleasure principle and happiness for others is a major theme.

Bentham's Life

Jeremy Bentham (1748–1832) was born in London, England, to a wealthy family whom he amazed with his outstanding genius. When he was only three years old, he read an eight-volume history of England. At four, he studied Latin grammar, and at eight, he went to Westminster School, one of Great Britain's leading boys' schools. At 12, Bentham entered Oxford University where he graduated with a bachelor of arts degree three years later.

Bentham's father wanted him to become a lawyer, but when Jeremy attended a lecture series on law given by the scholar Sir William Blackstone, the younger Bentham felt disgust with the power that the legal system used to oppress those beneath them. He dropped law and turned to a literary career. Bentham wrote commentaries on the need to create laws for the good of the general community, not just for the rich and powerful. Some people agreed with Bentham, but church authorities, lawyers, members of Parliament, and wealthy businessmen saw him as their foe.

Throughout his life, Bentham was a significant public figure. In an odd way, he continues to remain a public figure even today. His fully dressed, mummified body, complete with a wax head, is on display in a wooden cabinet in the main building of University College in London. Bentham had left a huge estate to the newly founded college, the first English university to admit students regardless of race, creed, or political belief, on the condition—according to legend—that he would continue to attend meetings of the university council even after his death.

Principle of Utility

In his major work, *Introduction to the Principles of Morals and Legislation*, Bentham wrote that pleasure and pain are the motivating factors of all human beings. The book begins with his view of human nature:

> 1. Nature has placed mankind under the governance of two sovereign masters, *pain* and *pleasure*. It is for them alone to point out what we ought to do, as well as to determine what we shall do. On the one hand the

Jeremy Bentham left instructions to be followed after his death that his body parts and skeleton be preserved, then dressed in his usual clothes, and put in his usual chair. This is Bentham's mummified body on display at University College in London.

standard of right and wrong, on the other the chain of causes and effects, are fastened to their throne. They govern us in all we do, in all we say, in all we think: every effort we can make to throw off our subjection, will serve but to demonstrate and confirm it. In words a man may pretend to abjure their empire: but in reality he will remain subject to it all the while. The *principle of utility* recognizes this subjection, and assumes it for the foundation of that system, the object of which is to rear the fabric of felicity by the hands of reason and law. Systems which attempt to question it, deal in sounds instead of sense, in caprice instead of reason, in darkness instead of light.[1]

Bentham's opinion that pleasure brings happiness is a philosophy of utility known as hedonism. For Bentham, there are two types of utilitarian hedonism: (1) psychological hedonism, meaning pleasure and pain determine what we do; and (2) ethical hedonism, meaning that pleasure is the only good, and actions are good only if they give us pleasure.

According to Bentham, whether we admit it or not, we are all hedonists—we all seek pleasure. Bentham, however, changed the conventional idea of hedonism to include happiness for the greatest number of people. Utility, he said, is that which produces pleasure, good, or happiness, not only for the individual but also for the whole community. For him, the word *good* meant "pleasure," and the word *pain* was the same as "evil."

Bentham argued that all moral standards are standards of pleasure. He said we do not obey the moral law out of a sense of duty; we obey the moral law because obeying it will bring us more pleasure than disobeying it. When asked, "Don't we obey the moral law to please God?" Bentham answered, "No. How could you possibly know God's pleasure when God neither speaks nor writes to us?" We invent God's pleasure "by observing our own pleasure and calling it his," he claims.

Four Sources of Pleasure and Pain

For Bentham, there are four sources, or what he called "sanctions," of pleasure and pain: (1) physical; (2) political; (3) moral; and (4) religious. In his view, a sanction means that, if we ignore the interests and pleasures of other people, we will feel pain.

> A man's goods, or his person, are consumed by fire. If this happened to him by what is called an accident, it was a calamity: if by reason of his own imprudence (for instance, from his neglecting to put his candle out) it may be styled a punishment of the physical sanction: if it happened to him by the sentence of a political magistrate, a punishment belonging to the political sanction; that is, what is commonly called a punishment: if for want of any assistance which his *neighbour* withheld from him out of some dislike to his *moral* character, a punishment of the *moral* sanction: if by an intermediate act of *God's* displeasure, manifested on account of some *sin* committed by him, or through any distraction of mind, occasioned by the dread of such displeasure, a punishment of the *religious* sanction. [2]

Bentham wanted to discover which sources of pleasure and pain would most likely give a society the most happiness. Bentham believed that morality depends not on the motives of our acts but on the consequences of our acts. The consequence of performing a moral act is pleasure. In society, if you inflict pain on others, the law punishes you, no matter what your motive. Motives, said Bentham, are important, but consequences are far more important. Painful consequences would punish our selfishness.

The Hedonic Calculus

Bentham believed that all people want to experience pleasure and avoid pain, but we need to realize there are different elements of pleasure. They are:

1. *Intensity. How strong is the pleasure?*
2. *Duration. How long would the pleasure last?*
3. *Certainty. How sure are we that the pleasure will occur?*
4. *Propinquity. How soon will the pleasure occur?*
5. *Fecundity. How likely is it that this pleasure will produce another pleasure?*
6. *Purity. How free from pain is the pleasure?*
7. *Extent. How many people will experience the pleasure?*

Bentham called the seven categories "the calculus of felicity [pleasure]." He thought that, by using these categories, we could calculate the action that would produce the greatest amount of happiness. The calculation would tell us the action we should morally take. In other words, we should ask ourselves these seven questions before reaching a decision. The calculus of felicity is also known as the hedonic calculus.

According to Bentham, if the totals are on the side of pleasure, then your choice is good. If the numbers favor the pain side, then your choice is bad. The quantity of pleasure is the important thing. Quantity of pleasure means if you and your friends get a greater amount of pleasure splashing around in the rain than going to the opera, then you should splash around in the rain. You only need to be sure that your pleasurable actions do not cause pain for anyone else.

Bentham's desire to construct a society that would provide the greatest happiness to the greatest number was the beginning of utilitarian philosophy.

JOHN STUART MILL

One of Bentham's most famous supporters, John Stuart Mill, was raised on an "educational experiment" worked out by his father and Bentham. Mill was deeply influenced by Bentham's philosophy. In fact, reading Bentham's ideas on the "greatest happiness principle" was one of the turning points of Mill's life.

Mill's Life

John Stuart Mill (1806–1873) was born in London, the oldest of nine children. James Mill, his father, was a famous philosopher and supporter of Jeremy Bentham. Following a plan he and Bentham devised, James Mill had his son John reading Greek at age three and reading Latin at eight. By the time John Mill was ten, he had read many of Plato's works on philosophy. Each morning, John and his father went on a walk, at which time his father would quiz him on the subjects he had studied the day before. Because of the intensity and strictness of this type of schooling, John Stuart Mill later said he had a quarter-of-a-century advantage over his peers, but sadly said, "I was never a boy."

When James Mill finished writing a history of India, he received a government position as an assistant examiner at the East India House in London. The East India House was responsible for the governing of India (then an English colony), and overseeing all correspondence and documents between the two nations. Five years later, James hired his son John, who was then 17, to work for him. John worked for the East India House for the next 34 years. At age 20, however, he had a nervous breakdown, which he blamed on too much analytic education and too few emotional outlets.

> I was . . . left stranded at the commencement of my voyage, with a well equipped ship and a rudder, but no sail;

without any real desire for the ends which I had been so carefully fitted out to work for; no delight in virtue or the general good, but also just as little in anything else. [3]

I seemed to have nothing left to live for. At first I hoped that the cloud would pass away of itself; but it did not. A night's sleep, the sovereign remedy for the smaller vexations of life, had no effect upon it. In vain I sought relief from my favourite books, those memorials of past nobleness and greatness from which I had always hitherto drawn strength and animation. I read them now without feeling . . . and I became persuaded that my love of mankind, and of excellence for its own sake, had worn itself out. [4]

To help nurture his feelings, John read the works of literary figures such as Samuel Coleridge, Thomas Carlyle, and William Wordsworth. Their writings helped him get in touch with his feelings and contributed to the development of his own moral philosophy.

At age 25, Mill met and became good friends with Harriet Taylor, the wife of a successful businessman. Taylor was a significant influence on Mill's ideas, especially being a source of his liberal views on feminism. Other than his father, Mill viewed Taylor as his life's chief intellectual influence and also one who had insight into the feeling aspect of human nature. John Mill wrote about the abstract and scientific, and Taylor wrote about the human aspect. They became a team, and, in 1851, two years after her husband's death, they married.

Seven years later, they moved to Avignon, France, but Harriet was in poor health and soon died. Mill continued to write, and over the next seven years, he published some of his most influential philosophy. In 1865, Mill returned to England and was elected to Parliament where he worked for women's rights. He was among the founders of the first women's suffrage society, helped with Irish land reform, and defended the rights of blacks in Jamaica. He returned to France to finish his *Autobiography* and died there at age 67.

Mill's Utilitarianism

At first, Mill wanted to defend Jeremy Bentham's principle of utility, but in the course of his defense, he began to worry about Bentham's hedonic calculus that said pleasures differ only in quantity or amount. Bentham had said that the "game of push-pin" has the same value as the arts and sciences, music, and poetry. Therefore, if the game of push-pin gives one more pleasure than the arts and sciences, it is more valuable, said Bentham. Mill, however, could not accept that the only difference between one act and another is the *amount* of pleasure we get. In his own life, Mill had discovered that all pleasures are not equal.

For Mill, there is also the *quality* of pleasure. For example, there is a qualitative pleasure in just being human that is superior to any of the quantitative pleasures experienced by animals such as pigs, or rats, or toads. "It is better," he said, "to be a human being dissatisfied than a pig satisfied."

> Few human creatures would consent to be changed into any of the lower animals, for a promise of the fullest allowance of a beast's pleasures; no intelligent human being would consent to be a fool, no instructed person would be an ignoramus, no person of feeling and conscience would be selfish and base, even though they should be persuaded that the fool, the dunce, or the rascal is better satisfied with his lot than they are with theirs. . . .

John Stuart Mill's writing includes works in social and political philosophy, logic, economics, ethics, religion, metaphysics, and current affairs. Throughout his life, Mill attempted to analyze and address important intellectual cultural movements of his time.

A being of higher faculties. . . . Can never really wish to sink into what he feels to be a lower grade of existence. . . . It is better to be a human being dissatisfied than a pig satisfied; better to be Socrates dissatisfied than a fool satisfied. And if the fool, or the pig, are of a different opinion, it is because they only know their own side of the question. The other party to the comparison knows both sides. [5]

Although we cannot measure quality, we know that one kind of pleasure always outshines the other in quality, and is therefore better. By suggesting that quality of pleasure is more desirable to humans than the quantity of pleasure, Mill rejected Bentham's notion.

Moral Philosophy

Bentham said we should choose acts that give us the greatest quantity of pleasure, and one of those acts is helping others. Mill agreed that helping others gives us pleasure because helping others includes the quality of altruism, or the unselfish concern for the welfare of others. For Mill, altruism emphasizes the Golden Rule: Treat others as you would have them treat you.

> The utilitarian morality does recognize in human beings the power of sacrificing their own greatest good for the good of others. . . .
>
> [T]he happiness which forms the utilitarian standard of what is right in conduct, is not the agent's own happiness, but that of all concerned. As between his own happiness and that of others, utilitarianism requires him to be as strictly impartial as a disinterested and benevolent spectator. In the golden rule of Jesus of Nazareth, we read the complete spirit of the ethics of utility. To do as you would be done by, and to love your neighbour as yourself, constitute the ideal perfection of utilitarian morality. [6]

Mill argued that our desire to be in unity with our fellow creatures helps civilizations make progress. Granting that each of us has a right to happiness, when we act altruistically, we want the greatest amount of happiness for the greatest number of people.

Education

For Mill, education is particularly important. Education teaches the skills that we need to live healthy and dignified lives. He believed that, with education, citizens of goodwill could eliminate poverty and lessen disease. People of "fortunate means" would find more happiness in helping the less fortunate than they would find in selfishly "caring for nobody but themselves." Mill wrote, "When people who are tolerably fortunate in their outward lot do not find in life sufficient enjoyment to make it valuable to them, the cause generally is, caring for nobody but themselves." [7]

Human Liberty

For Mill, we must have unlimited freedom of expression. Practicing the principle of the greatest good for the greatest number, he thought citizens should be free to criticize their government, to choose their own lifestyle, and to worship as they please.

> Human liberty. It comprises, first the inward domain of consciousness; demanding liberty of conscience in the most comprehensive sense; liberty of thought and feeling; absolute freedom of opinion and sentiment on all subjects, practical or speculative, scientific, moral, or theological. . . .
>
> Secondly, the principle requires liberty of tastes and pursuits; of framing the plan of our life to suit our own character; of doing as we like, subject to such consequences as may follow: without impediment from our fellow creatures, so long as what we do does not harm them, even though they should think our conduct foolish, perverse, or wrong. [8]

Mill argued that we must be free to express our thoughts. If we never challenge the opinions of others, including governments and religious institutions, we allow ourselves to depend upon someone else's authority. When that happens, the public tends toward conformity.

Women's Rights

Mill was a passionate defender of women's rights, and he believed both sexes should be involved in the political process. Together, he and Harriet Taylor questioned the English law of their day that proscribed that all women should marry but that no married woman could have property. All property, including her children, belonged to her husband. If a woman's husband died, she could not become the legal guardian of their children unless he requested it in his will. If the woman left her husband for any reason, she could take nothing with her, not even her children. If necessary, her husband could force her to return.

Because women were thought to lack intelligence, they could neither vote nor run for Parliament. Looked on as lesser beings than men, women were taught that virtue meant submission and meekness to their male "superiors." Men considered women best suited for domestic jobs.

Mill and Taylor argued that women should have independence, freedom to make their own choices, and freedom to get a good education. Society should view women as individuals in their own right, not existing as only relative to men, and men should stop defining the nature of women to women.

LINKS TO THE INDIVIDUAL

Utilitarianism influenced England for more than 100 years, mainly because utilitarian philosophers were so practical in their belief that people should search for pleasure and happiness. Yet, an antiutilitarianism philosophy, based on the individual and not on society as a whole, soon developed. This philosophy opposed the utilitarian notion of happiness for the masses by emphasizing the individual. For these thinkers, the self-reliant person is far more important than the happiness of the masses. Called "individualist" philosophers, they also rejected the utilitarian view that pleasure is the basis for moral values. Two of the leading individualist philosophers were Søren Kierkegaard and Friedrich Nietzsche.

2

THE INDIVIDUAL
Kierkegaard and Nietzsche

The Crowd is untruth.
—Søren Kierkegaard

A FORK IN THE ROAD

Although many earlier systems of philosophy had exerted a strong impact on religion and civilization, a new trend was about to begin. True, the utilitarians had looked forward to a social progress that would benefit everyone. Yet, some philosophers wondered if past thinkers truly understood the conflicts that we as individuals experience in our daily lives. Søren Kierkegaard and Friedrich Nietzsche were two such philosophers.

For Kierkegaard and Nietzsche, philosophy needed to take a different direction—the way of the individual. They wanted to do away with systems that claimed to have worked out a total understanding of humanity and history. They wanted to stress the idea that individuals are free to choose their own paths. Humans, they insisted, do not have a fixed nature as other animals and plants do. Humans create their own nature by the choices they make. Even our refusal to choose is a choice. We are free to create who we become, they argued.

Philosophy was about to take a fork in the road. Spurred by the thinking of Kierkegaard and Nietzsche, philosophy was about to make a shift from viewing humanity objectively as objects or property, to viewing humanity subjectively, as subjects, or individual human beings.

SØREN KIERKEGAARD

Kierkegaard, known as the Father of Existentialism, was the first philosopher to reject giant philosophical systems in favor of understanding the human situation. He believed that, even in the face of anxiety, fear, and guilt, we must live a totally committed life. We must be true to ourselves, even if that means defying the norms of society. A devout Christian who belonged to no church, Kierkegaard believed the highest commitment we can make is to experience God through what he called the "leap of faith." Only this commitment could save us from despair.

Kierkegaard's Life

Born in Copenhagen, Denmark, Søren Kierkegaard (1813–1855) was the youngest of seven children. His father, Michael, grew up as a poor peasant, and his mother, Anne, had been a servant. While his father was a young man, he had angrily cursed God for his family's poverty. For the rest of his life, Michael never forgave himself for his outburst against God. Although Michael was often depressed, he worked hard and became an influential merchant. Søren was also a melancholy person and often depressed. Michael raised Søren and his siblings in a strict Christian atmosphere, and, like James Mill, he put his son through rigorous intellectual homeschooling.

When Søren was 17, his father enrolled him at the University of Copenhagen to study theology and become a minister. Kierkegaard, however, soon discovered that his intellectual interests were in philosophy and literature. While in college, his

sensuous desires caught fire and his studies took a backseat
to having fun. He spent huge sums of money on food, drink,
clothes, and socializing. He was always popular at parties, but
his escapades often threw him into deep depression. After one
party, he wrote in his journal:

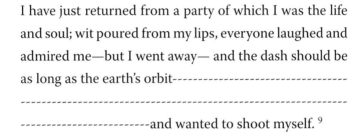

> I have just returned from a party of which I was the life
> and soul; wit poured from my lips, everyone laughed and
> admired me—but I went away— and the dash should be
> as long as the earth's orbit------------------------------------
> --
> -----------------------and wanted to shoot myself. [9]

Four days after his twenty-fifth birthday, Kierkegaard experienced a religious conversion that gave him "indescribable joy."
The experience was so powerful that he gave up his partying
life and returned to studying theology. Two years later, he fell
in love with a 14-year-old girl, Regine Olsen. They became engaged, but a few months later, over her protests, he broke their
engagement. It was one of the most difficult things he ever did,
but he felt that he must live a "life wholly dedicated to God."

Two weeks after ending their relationship, Kierkegaard went
to Berlin, Germany, where he spent most of his time writing.
While there, he decided to reconcile with Regine, but she had
become engaged to a former boyfriend. In severe depression,
Kierkegaard compared his sacrifice of his love for Regine to
Abraham's offering of his son Isaac's life to God, in the Old Tes-
tament (see Genesis 22). Kierkegaard thought about the choice
he had to make: "Either devote my life to God or live in comfort
with Regine." In the Bible story, God spared Isaac's life. Kierkegaard questioned why God did not save his life with Regine. After much soul-searching, he decided that no universal principle
could be applied to such situations. There are only individual

predicaments. It must be God's will that he lost Regine. Yet what did God expect him to do? Perplexed, Kierkegaard wrote:

> What I really lack is to be clear in my mind *what I am to do,* not what I am to know, except in so far as certain understanding must precede every action. The thing is to understand myself, to see what God really wishes *me* to do; the thing is to find a truth which is true *for me,* to find *the idea for which I can live and die.* [10]

After another powerful spiritual experience, Kierkegaard took his leap of faith and spent the rest of his life in a brilliant literary career. He died at the early age of 42.

The Existing Individual

An eager student, Kierkegaard studied the great philosophers, but he came to different conclusions. For instance, Plato thought if we know universal Forms, especially the Form of the Good, then we would do good. Kierkegaard disagreed. Whether we know the good or not, he said, we still have to make hard choices. Kierkegaard insisted that humans are actors in the drama of our existence. No matter what is the universal scheme of things, we have to make important decisions every day of our lives. We cannot mold our precious and mysterious lives into a logical system. To truly exist as individuals, we must have passion and commitment.

> It is impossible to exist without passion. . . . Every Greek thinker was therefore essentially a passionate thinker. I have often reflected how one might bring a man into a state of passion. I have thought in this connection that if I could get him seated on a horse and the horse made to take flight and gallop wildly, or better still, for the sake

For Søren Kierkegaard, the primary characteristic of human beings is that we stand out as responsible individuals who make free choices and take a "leap of faith," even if we can never know with certainty the outcome of our choices.

of bringing the passion out, if I could take a man who wanted to arrive at a certain place as quickly as possible, and hence already had some passion, and could set him astride a horse that can scarcely walk—and yet this is what existence is like if one is to become consciously aware of it. Or if a driver were otherwise not especially inclined toward passion, if someone hitched a team of horses to a wagon for him, one of them a Pegasus and the other a worn-out jade, and told him to drive—I think one might succeed. And it is just this that it means to exist, if one is to become conscious of it. Eternity is the winged horse, infinitely fast, and time is a worn-out jade; the existing individual is the driver.[11]

Kierkegaard used the example of two kinds of men driving a wagon. One man holds the reins but is asleep. The other man holds the reins and is fully awake. In the first case, the horse goes along the familiar road without any direction from the sleeping driver. In the other case, the man is awake and truly driving the horse. Surely, both men exist, but Kierkegaard believed that existence must refer to a *quality* in the individual; namely, his conscious participation in an act. Only the conscious driver truly exists.

To exist, said Kierkegaard, implies a certain kind of individual who strives, who considers alternatives, who chooses, who decides, and who, above all, commits himself. To exist means to be aware, subjectively, or inwardly, of our unique individuality.

Kierkegaard agreed that we could solve some problems by using objective principles such as mathematics and science as well as ethics and metaphysics. Yet, life also makes demands upon us, and at these critical moments, logical thought does not always solve problems. To prove his point, Kierkegaard asked us to take a look at the biblical story of Abraham in which God said to the aged man, "Take your son, your only son, Isaac, whom you love, and . . . offer him up as a burnt offering." Kierkegaard asked if universal principles or empirical science could help Abraham decide whether to obey God and sacrifice his son. Like Abraham, we all face situations that force us to become aware of ourselves. Important truths are personal, not scientific or metaphysical.

The Fall

According to Kierkegaard, we exist in the world because we have fallen from our essential self (Figure 1), which is our immortal relationship to God, into an existential condition of anxiety and eventually death, which is our alienation from God.

Kierkegaard believed that we all have the inner drive to find our essential self, although mathematics and science cannot bridge the gap between ourselves and God. The only way to regain our relationship with God is through the leap of faith.

Without faith, our actions only drive us even further from God into deeper alienation and despair. Sensing our own insecurity, we then try to do something. For example, we might try to find some meaning in our lives by losing ourselves in a crowd, such as a church, a political party, a club, or a team sport. In a crowd, we feel safe because we do not have to take individual responsibility for the outcome of an action. Yet, losing ourselves in a crowd will not work, said Kierkegaard, because "a crowd

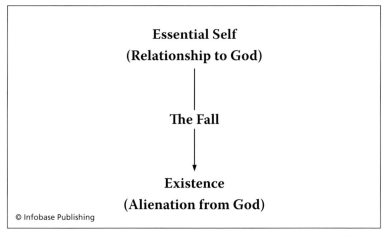

Figure 1. Kierkegaard's concept of humankind's existence. The fall from our essential self casts us into our current existence, an alienation from God.

in its very concept is the untruth. . . . It renders the individual completely impenitent and irresponsible."

For Kierkegaard, the real solution is to relate ourselves to God rather than to groups of people. Until we do this, our lives will be full of anxiety. Because the root of our anxieties is our alienation from God, these anxieties create in us a dynamic drive to find our essential self. Kierkegaard explained this dynamic drive as the "stages on life's way."

The Stages on Life's Way

Looking at his own experiences, Kierkegaard determined that there are three stages in life: (1) the aesthetic stage; (2) the ethical stage; and (3) the religious stage. He believed these three stages represent three ways of making choices in our lives.

Aesthetic Stage.   The aesthetic, or sensuous, stage is the lowest stage on life's way. The individual lives for selfish pleasure and refuses to make commitments. Life is a whim, full of gusto, instant satisfaction, and self-gratification. Everything at this stage is for the pleasure of the moment. Whether eating, playing computer games, snowboarding, or being the life of the party, the aesthetic individual is completely absorbed in instant pleasure. A person at this stage lives to escape boredom because "boredom is the root of all evil."

> This can be traced back to the very beginning of the world. The gods were bored; therefore they created human beings. Adam was bored because he was alone; therefore Eve was created. . . . Adam was bored alone; then Adam and Eve were bored together; then Adam and Eve and Cain and Abel were bored *en famille.* After that, the population of the world increased and the nations were bored *en masse.* To amuse themselves, they hit upon the notion of building a tower [the Tower of Babel] so high that it would

reach the sky. This notion is just as boring as the tower was high and is a terrible demonstration of how boredom had gained the upper hand. [12]

Once boredom sets in, said Kierkegaard, the aesthetic person falls into despair. No one can live in the aesthetic stage without falling into despair. Realizing the meaninglessness of life, the dialectical process sets in, and the individual's thinking becomes a serious "either/or" conflict. "Either I stay where I am, or I choose a different lifestyle." For Kierkegaard, this is more than a rational choice. It is an act of will—a commitment to become a better person. Knowledge of science, mathematics, or the structure of the universe cannot help one make this choice. This is a personal choice based on "fear and trembling," according to Kierkegaard.

Ethical Stage   In the ethical stage, life becomes more serious. Moral standards replace sensuous pleasures, and selfishness gives way to responsibility. In the ethical stage, individuals accept certain rules set by society. For instance, if we are in the ethical stage, we may want to kick back and watch television or hang out with friends, but we go to school or to work instead. Reaching beyond our own selfish pleasures, we develop strong opinions on moral issues such as abortion, capital punishment, the right to die, and same-sex marriages. Unlike the aesthetic, whose only concern is whether something is gratifying or boring, in the ethical stage we try to follow moral laws. We consider it a duty to follow moral laws.

Although the ethical stage is much higher than the aesthetic stage, it is not the highest stage in which we can live. No matter how moral we are, or how important our moral opinions are, said Kierkegaard, the ethical stage is not enough. In this stage, we still feel alienation from God, which causes us feelings of despair, emptiness, and guilt. At this point, the either/or dialectic process begins to work deep within our consciousness. Either we stay secure in the ethical stage, or by an act of will, we take the leap of faith.

Religious Stage   Because the religious stage calls for the deepest commitment a person can make, Kierkegaard considered it the highest stage. The religious stage is not the same as attending religious services. We would do that in the ethical stage. The religious stage is between you and God. No one knows what God may command, and this not knowing is why Kierkegaard called this stage the "leap of faith." To explain, he referred once again to Abraham. Obeying God's command, Abraham sadly agreed to sacrifice his son Isaac. As Abraham lifted the knife to take his son's life, an angel stopped him and offered a sacrificial goat in Isaac's place.

The leap of faith, insisted Kierkegaard, is not rational. Rather, it is absurd. How was Abraham to make the decision to sacrifice his beloved son to God? He could not rely on the moral codes of his tribe or his culture. His people would say, "Killing your son is murder!" Nothing could help Abraham except his faith in God, and he could answer to no one but God. That is why the leap of faith is so difficult: It is a passionate commitment to God. Yet, only in the religious stage can the leap of faith take us into our true, essential self in a relationship with God. "Without risk there is no faith," said Kierkegaard.

FRIEDRICH NIETZSCHE

Another philosopher who stressed the unique individual was Friedrich Nietzsche. He agreed with Kierkegaard that we must find our true self, but for Nietzsche, it was not in God. For Nietzsche, "God is dead and we have killed him." The true self is in the human being, he claims. Nietzsche, however, believed that most humans are "bungled and botched," and, therefore, have no inkling of a true self. Furthermore, because the masses follow the "herd mentality," they have no original thoughts of their own. They merely "pick up the excrement of great minds."

If you want to be a unique individual, said Nietzsche, you must follow your conscience, which shouts, "Be yourself! You are not really all that which you do, think, and desire now."

Nietzsche's Life

Friedrich Wilhelm Nietzsche (1844–1900) was born in Röcken, Prussia (present-day Germany), and was named after the Prussian king Friedrich Wilhelm, whose birthday he shared. Nietzsche's father was a Lutheran minister, and his mother was the daughter of a Lutheran minister. When Nietzsche was five years old, his father died of "softening of the brain." Nietzsche spent his childhood in a household of women, which included his mother, his grandmother, his sister, and two aunts.

After grade school, Nietzsche attended boarding school and was an outstanding student in the classics, literature, and religion. While there, he read Plato and other Greek scholars. Although his genius was evident, he suffered migraine headaches, insomnia, upset stomach, and bad eyesight. These ailments remained with him throughout life.

In 1864, Nietzsche attended the University of Bonn, Germany, to study theology and classical philology, or the study of literary texts. One year later, he attended the University of Leipzig, where he discovered the philosophy of Arthur Schopenhauer and gave up religion. Nietzsche's work was so impressive that, even before completing his doctorate degree, the University of Basel in Switzerland offered him the head professorship of classical philology. The University of Leipzig immediately awarded him a doctorate degree without examination or dissertation, and within a year, the University of Basel promoted him to full professor.

Ten years after receiving the professorship, Nietzsche's poor health forced him to resign. He traveled through Italy, Switzerland, and Germany searching desperately, yet unsuccessfully, for a place to regain his health. During those years, he wrote his major philosophical works.

After writing book after book with amazing speed, Nietzsche suffered a mental breakdown. One day, while walking in Turin, Italy, he saw a man beating his horse so severely that the horse collapsed to the ground. Nietzsche ran to the scene, knelt down, and threw his arms around the horse's neck. By the time officials had pulled him away, however, his mind had snapped. For the last 11 years of his life, Nietzsche's insanity kept him from completing his last major work, the *Revaluation of All Values.*

"GOD IS DEAD"

In one of the most famous passages in philosophy, Nietzsche pronounced the death of God, claiming, "God is dead, and you and I have killed him. Who will wipe this blood off us?" Nietzsche condemned nineteenth-century Europe, claiming that, despite feeling secure in its strong military power and material wealth, the moral values of the continent had collapsed. Nietzsche saw in Europe the belief that the universe had no purpose and that life is meaningless. People had destroyed their faith in God, yet were blind to the fact that they had killed him. Could it be prophetic that Nietzsche put his famous words, "God is dead," from his work *The Gay Science*, into the mouth of a character called "the madman"?

> *The Madman*—Have you not heard of that madman who lit a lantern in the bright morning hours, ran to the market place, and cried incessantly: "I seek God! I seek God!"—As many of those who did not believe in

God were standing around just then, he provoked much laughter. Has he got lost? asked one. Did he lose his way like a child? asked another. Or is he hiding? Is he afraid of us? Has he gone on a voyage? Emigrated?—Thus they yelled and laughed.

The madman jumped into their midst and pierced them with his eyes. "Whither is God?" he cried; "I will tell you. *We have killed him*—you and I. All of us are his murderers. But how did we do this? How could we drink up the sea? Who gave us the sponge to wipe away the entire horizon? . . . Do we hear nothing as yet of the noise of the grave diggers who are burying God? Do we smell nothing as yet of the divine decomposition? Gods, too, decompose. God is dead. God remains dead. And we have killed him.

"How shall we comfort ourselves, the murderers of all murderers? What was holiest and mightiest of all that the world has yet owned has bled to death under our knives: who will wipe this blood off us. . . . Is not the greatness of this deed too great for us? Must we ourselves not become gods simply to appear worthy of it? There has never been a greater deed; and whoever is born after us—for the sake of this deed he will belong to a higher history than all history hitherto."

Here the madman fell silent and looked again at his listeners; and they, too, were silent and stared at him in astonishment. At last he threw his lantern on the ground, and it broke into pieces and went out. "I have come too early," he said then; "My time is not yet. This tremendous event is still on its way, still wandering; it has not yet reached the ears of men. Lightning and thunder require time; the light of the stars requires time; deeds, though done, still require time to be seen and heard. This deed is still more distant from them than the most distant stars—*and yet they have done it themselves."*

It has been related further that on the same day the madman forced his way into several churches and there struck up his *requiem aeternam deo* [requiem to God]. Led out and called to account, he is said always to have replied nothing but: "What after all are these churches now if they are not the tombs and sepulchers of God?"[13]

For Nietzsche, the death of God was the fault of the churches. People became part of the "herd mentality" by looking to the authority of the church for all their answers to life. Instead, they should have relied on themselves. Yet, Nietzsche viewed the loss of belief in God as the way for unique individuals to develop fully. The Christian god, with his commands and judgments, no longer stood in the way. The death of God meant freedom:

> Indeed, we philosophers and "free spirits" feel, when we hear the news that "the old god is dead," as if a new dawn shone on us; our heart overflows with gratitude, amazement, premonitions, expectation. At long last the horizon appears free to us again, even if it should not be bright; at long last our ships may venture out again, venture out to face any danger; all the daring of the lover of knowledge is permitted again; the sea, *our* sea, lies open again; perhaps there has never yet been such an "open sea."[14]

Under Christianity, said Nietzsche, what the masses call "good" is not virtue, and what the masses call "truth" is selfishness. Furthermore, religion is a psychological weapon with which "moral pygmies domesticate natural giants." True values, he said, will come to light only when we take off the mask of modern morality. The mask covers the weakness of the masses that look to authority for answers instead of looking within themselves.

Master and Slave Morality

Based on his observations of human beings, Nietzsche discovered two types of morality: master morality and slave morality (Figure 2). In the master morality, good and bad are the same as noble and despicable. In the slave morality, the standard is utility, or that which is helpful to the society of the weak and powerless.

For Nietzsche, the noble man of master morality creates his own values out of the abundance of his life and strength. He represents the movement of ascending life. The "herd mentality" of slave morality represents inferior life, descending life, and degeneracy. Those in the slave morality see virtue in such things as sympathy, kindness, and humility. By their

Master Morality	Slave Morality
1. A noble soul.	1. "Bungled and botched."
2. Regards himself as creator and determines his own values.	2. Lowest elements of society; (the abused, the oppressed, and those who are uncertain of themselves).
3. He does not look outside himself for approval. He is his own judge.	3. Goodness symbolizes the qualities of sympathy; pity; kind, helping hand; warm heart, humility, patience.
4. He acts out of a feeling of power.	4. Morality of utility. Benefits the weak and powerless.
5. He may help the unfortunate, but not out of pity—out of abundance of power.	5. Morality based on resentment. Fear the master.
6. He is self-disciplined.	6. Mediocre values.
7. Natural leaders.	7. Natural followers.
© Infobase Publishing	

Figure 2. A comparison of Nietzsche's master and slave moralities.

Friedrich Nietzsche challenged traditional morality and religion, believing in creativity and the realities of our world we live in, rather than the promises of a world beyond.

standards, the strong and independent individuals are danger-ous, and, therefore, evil. Slave morality applies to the masses—Nietzsche's "bungled and botched"—because its values express the needs of a herd. Being meek and powerless, those in the slave morality fear unique and powerful individuals, and so they insist that their herd values are the absolute truth. Slave morality begins with resentment, which is not acknowledged by the herd. In fact, the herd is not even aware that they resent unique individuals.

Nietzsche always referred to individuals in the master morality as "he." Nietzsche saw no virtue in women. Of women, he said, "They are not, as yet, capable of friendships; they are still cats, or birds, or at the best, cows. Man shall be trained for war and women for the recreation of the warrior. All else is folly." And Nietzsche warns the warrior: "Thou goest to woman? Do not forget thy whip."

Nietzsche believed the master morality and the slave morality could coexist if the herd was content to keep its mediocre values to itself. Unfortunately, it does not do that. Instead, the herd tries to impose its own values on everyone. Nietzsche saw Christianity in the West as an example of the herd mentality. "I regard Christianity as the most fatal and seductive lie that has ever yet existed. . . . It seeks to keep alive life's failures—the defective, the diseased, and the suffering individuals." By directing a Christian's thinking toward God instead of toward man, Christianity weakens the powerful energies in the strong person. Nietzsche did, however, admire Jesus as a unique individual. His harsh criticisms of religion were directed against the churches.

Will to Power

Nietzsche rejected all moral systems. "People are different," he said. The only thing all people have in common is "the will to power." The will to power expresses itself everywhere and in everything. Even our motives have their roots in the will to power. Both the master and the slave morality have their roots in power, but each uses power differently. There is one set of virtues for the masters and another set for the slaves.

The Superman

The ideal person, Nietzsche said, is the "superman." The superman is as far beyond the ordinary person as the ordinary person is beyond the monkey (Figure 3).

Supermen are the few rare individuals who become masters of themselves, controlling their passions, their powers, and their weaknesses. For Nietzsche, the superman is the goal of human nature. The bungled and the botched ordinary person is a condition to overcome.

> Man is a rope, tied between beast and overman [superman]—a rope over an abyss. A dangerous across, a dangerous on-the-way, a dangerous looking-back, a dangerous shuddering and stopping.
>
> What is great in man is that he is a bridge and not an end; what can be loved in man is that he is an *overture* and a *going under*.[15]

The superman represents the highest level of physical, intellectual, and emotional development. To become the superman, you must organize your passions, give style to your

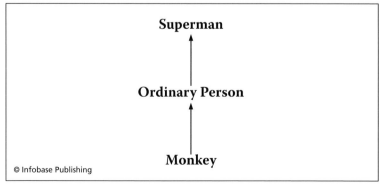

Figure 3. A diagram of Nietzsche's view of the relationship of superman, ordinary person, and a monkey.

character, and become creative. You must be conscious of life's terrors, yet affirm life, without resentment. One of life's terrors is that it has no meaning, except the meaning you give to your own life. You must raise yourself above the herd and cease being "human, all-too-human," in Nietzsche's words.

Whom did Nietzsche have in mind as the superman? "The Roman Caesar with Christ's soul," is one, he said. The literary great Johann Wolfgang Von Goethe, author of *Faust*, is another. Nietzsche also mentioned Alcibiades, an ancient Greek statesman and general; Alexander the Great; Italian Renaissance military leader and statesman Cesare Borgia; and Napoleon Bonaparte as examples of the superman. They had discipline, strength, courage, and creativity. Both Alexander the Great and Napoleon destroyed city-states and republics to create great empires. Yet Nietzsche most admired the powers of the artist and the philosopher. There is more power in self-control, art, and philosophy, he said, than in the conquest of others. The superman is the hero, an individual of intelligence, and a passionate person with creative discipline and self-control. The superman has the courage to say "Yes!" to life.

Eternal Recurrence

What if life eternally recurs, questioned Nietzsche. Would anyone, even the superman, have the courage to look at the possibility that life has no meaning and yet occurs over and over again? For example, if Earth were totally destroyed, would it eventually reconstruct and all of history repeat again?

If eternal recurrence is a fact, and God is dead, then we could never look for the meaning of life in a heavenly realm beyond death.

> *The greatest weight*—What, if some day or night a demon were to steal after you into your loneliest loneliness and say to you: "This life as you now live it and have

lived it, you will have to live once more and innumerable times more; and there will be nothing new in it, but every pain and every joy and every thought and sigh and everything unutterable small or great in your life will have to return to you, all in the same moonlight between the trees, and even the moment and I myself. The eternal hourglass of existence is turned up-side down again and again, and you with it, speck of dust!" [16]

Eternal recurrence suggests that this world would occur over and over again with no personal salvation. Nietzsche thought that only the strongest could bear this heavy weight, and only the superman could say "Yes!" to eternal recurrence. Why? Because, said Nietzsche, only the superman could truly love and affirm with joy Earth and his life.

LINKS TO CONTEMPORARY PHILOSOPHY

Before Kierkegaard and Nietzsche, much of philosophy focused on objective views of the universe and of the human mind and how it works. Although human beings were the objects of such systematic philosophy, we were viewed simply as human *objects* rather than human *beings*. After Kierkegaard and Nietzsche, however, philosophers began to look deeper into the value of human life and the importance of making personal decisions. They now looked into the nature of individuals—our anxieties, our guilt, and our power—our struggle for freedom to find our true self.

Thus was born the practical twentieth-century philosophy known as pragmatism.

3

PRAGMATISM
James and Dewey

As a rule we disbelieve all facts and theories
for which we have no use.
—William James

THE CONTEMPORARY WORLD

By the mid-nineteenth century, philosophers no longer looked to the ancient Greek, medieval, or modern philosophers to give them knowledge of ultimate reality. They argued that there was no ultimate knowledge of anything. They had also come to agree that no system of moral knowledge was possible. Lastly, contemporary philosophy lost its connection with the Jewish and Christian belief in an intelligent, holy, and powerful creator of the world. The notion of an absolute mind or will, or an absolute anything, seemed foreign to most Western philosophers of the twentieth century.

Part of the change in philosophical attitudes started at the beginning of the century as new discoveries in science were being made. Max Planck founded the quantum theory in physics, and Albert Einstein discovered the theory of relativity. Both theories seemed to imply the impossibility of objective and certain knowledge.

World War I

World War I (1914–1918) was another event that brought significant changes in philosophy and society. Prior to the war, Europeans and Americans felt confident in the progress of economics and technology. The horrors of the war, however, shattered that confidence, as over 40 million people worldwide were killed or wounded. Almost 10 million soldiers were killed, many by the destructive power of new weapons, such as the machine gun. Especially unsettling for most people was the idea that people of all nations had prayed to the same god for victory.

After the war, the distinction between social classes began to blur, and societies tended to become more democratic. The upper classes lost some of their power because soldiers of all classes had faced the same danger and horror in the trenches. Now, those who had bled and suffered for their country wanted a voice in running it.

As the demands for radical social and economic change grew, the Western powers began to experiment with socialist ideas within the capitalist system. People looked to their governments to provide things such as health care, the construction of roads and airports, social security, and the regulation of the economy. Workers, desiring to exert a greater voice in their lives, formed unions and rose to protect themselves from unfair labor practices. The failure of some of these changes in capitalism led to the great economic depression of the 1930s, which, in turn, was a principal cause of the next worldwide conflict.

World War II

World War II (1939–1945) began when Germany's dictator, Adolf Hitler, invaded Poland. Soon after the invasion, Great Britain and France declared war on Germany. The war years saw the death of more people, more destroyed property, and more disrupted lives than any other war in history. The estimated loss of life was roughly 72 million people throughout the world, including death due to famine and disease.

The war left Europe in ruins and cost Europe the intellectual, economic, and military superiority it had enjoyed since the sixteenth century. Yet, from the rubble of destruction, a new world began to emerge, a world in which class distinctions began to blur and technology impacted the lives of everyone everywhere. Information and entertainment became available to the average citizen almost worldwide. A common culture developed among the masses that lowered the standards of literature, music, and art. The masses generally showed little, if any, interest in the arts or philosophy. The average person, who had the time and money, was unwilling to spend either on higher culture. Art, literature, and music turned toward the few, away from the masses. European philosophers no longer wrote for the intelligent and cultured reader but only for other philosophers. Their vision narrowed, and they became more specific and more analytic.

In common-sense America, a school of practical philosophy, known as pragmatism, was putting down roots. Braving both world wars and economic turmoil, it grew and blossomed. Even today, America is known as a pragmatic, or practical, nation.

PRAGMATISM

Pragmatism was a uniquely American brand of philosophy that began at the end of the nineteenth century. Pragmatism holds that ideas are only useful if they can be put into action. Pragmatic philosophers tossed aside all thinking that had no practical value. Two of the leaders of this new age of practical thinking were William James, who popularized the new philosophy, and John Dewey, who introduced it into American schools.

Although James and Dewey lived at the same time and came from New England, each one expressed a different kind of pragmatism. James showed an interest in psychology and religion while Dewey focused on ethics and social studies. They agreed that truth is what works for us and what is useful in society. Unlike the ancient Greeks, Socrates and Plato, the pragmatists did not believe in an absolute unchanging Truth that applies to all people everywhere at all times.

WILLIAM JAMES

The pragmatists wanted to bridge the gap between several earlier schools of thinking, most notably the British empiricists and the traditional rationalists and idealists. For example, based on Charles Darwin's theory of evolution, empiricists saw humans as part of a biological process; namely, the survival of the fittest. Evolutionists believed that human beings are part of a natural mechanical process and are in no position to help direct history. The rationalists and idealists, such as René Descartes, Immanuel Kant, and Georg Wilhelm Hegel, held the opposite view of human nature. William James, the pragmatist, argued that empiricists and rationalists differed because of their temperaments. The rationalists are "tender-minded," and the empiricists are "tough-minded." He listed the differences between them in two columns (Figure 4).

According to James, the tough-minded viewed the tender-minded as "sentimentalists and soft-heads." The tender-minded viewed the tough-minded as "unrefined, callous, or brutal." James thought that most of us would desire the positive attributes of both groups.

James's Life

William James (1842–1910) was born in New York City to a wealthy and highly cultured family. He and his younger brother,

The Tender-Minded Rationalist	The Tough-Minded Empiricist
Theories and principles	Facts
Intellectual	Sensationalists
Idealists	Materialists
Optimists	Pessimists
Religious	Irreligious
Free will	Fatalists
Monists	Pluralists
Dogmatic	Skeptical

© Infobase Publishing

Figure 4. William James's comparison of the "tender-minded" rationalists and the "tough-minded" empiricists.

Henry, were born within 15 months of each other and were always close friends. Their father, Henry Sr., was a restless man, so William and his brother spent much of their youth moving from place to place. In 1855, when Henry Sr. lost faith in American education, he moved the family to Europe. William and Henry James received their formal education in private schools in England, France, Switzerland, and Germany before returning to America.

At an early age, Henry James decided on a writing career, and he eventually became a famous novelist. William James was not certain what he wanted as a profession, so he tried his hand at many things, such as art, chemistry, anatomy, and physiology. During his years as a student at Harvard, William suffered from a constant state of anxiety and depression. One day, he decided to get well, and he actually *willed* himself well. With this new attitude, his depression lifted like a veil. He graduated from Harvard in 1869 with a degree in medicine, but instead of going into practice, he found a new interest in psychology and philosophy. After graduation, James taught physiology, then psychology, and then philosophy at Harvard, where he remained for 36 years, his entire professional life.

In 1876, James met Alice Gibbens, a bright, honest young teacher. Two years later, they married. Although he still fought bouts of depression, Alice was a source of support and encouragement, and 13 years after their marriage, James published a two-volume *Principles of Psychology*; this work became widely acclaimed and won him invitations to lecture around the United States.

In 1898, James was invited to give the Gifford Lectures in Edinburgh, Scotland, a rare honor for an American. These lectures, which offered a wide range of his philosophy about religion, were published in 1902 as *The Varieties of Religious Experience*, a book that is as popular today as it was then.

He retired from Harvard in 1907 but continued to lecture and write, with all of his books becoming classics of American philosophy. In 1910, he sailed to Europe for treatments to cure his cardiac pain, a condition he had suffered for years. The treatments were unsuccessful, and James remarked that too much "sitting up and talking" with friends only weakened him further. That same year, he returned to his country home in New Hampshire to rest, but he died two days later. He was 68.

The Pragmatic Method

The term *pragmatism* comes from the Greek *pragma*, meaning "action." For James, action means "practice" or "practical." Thus, pragmatism is an inquiry into the practical meaning of ideas, events, and life itself. Pragmatism rejects rationalism as dogmatic because rationalism gives answers about our world with no application to life. How do we apply such a theory to our life, James asked. Pragmatism, on the other hand, looks at results. For example, if there is a dispute whether or not

God exists, pragmatism offers no definite answer, but it asks, "Does it work for you to believe in God?"

> The pragmatic method is primarily a method of settling metaphysical disputes that otherwise might be interminable. Is the world one or many?—fated or free?—material or spiritual?—here are notions either of which may or may not hold good of the world; and disputes over such notions are unending. The pragmatic method in such cases is to try to interpret each notion by tracing its respective practical consequences. What difference would it practically make to any one if this notion rather than that notion were true? If no practical difference whatever can be traced, then the alternatives mean practically the same thing, and all dispute is idle. Whenever a dispute is serious, we ought to be able to show some practical difference that must follow from one side or the other's being right. . . .
>
> A pragmatist turns his back resolutely and once for all upon a lot of inveterate habits dear to professional philosophers. He turns away from abstraction and insufficiency, from verbal solutions, from bad *a priori* reasons, from fixed principles, closed systems, and pretended absolutes and origins. He turns towards concreteness and adequacy, towards facts, towards action and towards power. [17]

True Ideas

James looked for what he called the "cash-value" of statements, or the practical payoff, and he rejected any philosophy that did not have it. For anything to be meaningful, it must in some way relate to our personal experience. For ideas to be true, they must make an actual, concrete difference in our lives.

William James was a pioneering thinker and prolific author in the fields of philosophy, psychology, and physiology. In 1890, he published his masterwork, *The Principles of Psychology*, which established him as the premier psychologist of his time.

Pragmatism . . . asks its usual question. "Grant an idea or belief to be true," it says, "what concrete difference will its being true make in any one's actual life? What experiences will be different from those which would obtain if the belief were false? What, in short, is the truth's cash-value in experiential terms?" [18]

Ideas, said James, are always changing. Therefore, they are true only when they relate to our own experiences. For example, very few people today consider it wrong for women to wear jeans in public, but not long ago, society considered it objectionable for women to wear jeans. Likewise, few people now consider it wrong for men to wear earrings, but this was not always the case. Religious ideas, like social ideas, also change. James thought religion is vital to human happiness, and he believed that, when old religions no longer "work," new religious ideas take their place.

James was keenly aware that society does not easily accept change, but when old ideas are no longer useful, we do give birth to new ideas. Ideas are accepted or rejected based on how well they work for us. Thus, pragmatism's test of truth is what works best.

James also believed that we create new truths and new ideas the same way we create health and wealth. Just as we benefit from staying healthy, we benefit by seeking the truth. Truth, said James, is a process in which we make ideas become true when we experience certain events.

Consciousness

We could say that James's moral philosophy was in part his answer to French philosopher René Descartes's mind-body problem. Descartes had identified two kinds of substance: mind and matter. Matter mechanically follows physical laws, and mind is free. Somehow, mind and body interact, or connect. Descartes believed that they interacted in the brain's pineal gland. This solution, however, was not particularly satisfactory for Descartes or for philosophers who came after him.

For James, the solution to the mind-body problem is consciousness. There is only a separation between mind and body when we believe that minds are conscious and bodies are unconscious. Yet, our mind is not separate from the body because there is only one substance in the world out of which everything is composed, and that substance is consciousness.

James disagreed with the British empiricists who said that we have no experience of a connection between things. For James, consciousness brings all the pieces of experience together. Nothing can be separated from consciousness.

Freedom

Freedom, as everything else, is a process of consciousness. We are free to make choices that could change the direction of our lives. The opposite of freedom is determinism. Determinism is the belief that everything that happens must happen exactly the way it does. When you eat an apple, you are not free to decide whether to digest the apple in your stomach or in your lungs. There are physical laws that leave you no choice but to digest the apple in your stomach.

It is true that physical laws are determined, but James thought that we are not made up of physical laws alone. We have free will. We can choose to eat the apple or not. In a deterministic world, our lives would have little meaning because we could not make choices at all. If we could not make choices, then moral responsibility becomes nonsense. There would be no reason to regret anything, even murder.

For James, if we lived in a deterministic world, our lives would have little meaning, but if freedom exists, then there is meaning in our lives. Is it even possible to imagine our lives without believing we have free will? James did not think so. For him, our thoughts, hopes, regrets, and actions are our own free choice. We judge actions such as lying, stealing, and murdering to be wrong. We say people who commit these acts could have made different choices. James could not conceive of a world where murder *must* happen. He saw this world as a place where murder *can* happen, but it *should not* happen. We are free to choose.

Morality and the Good Life

The question that faces all moral philosophers is, "How do we live the good life?" For James, before we could answer such a question, we must understand the meaning of good. When we look at animals or nature, we never judge them as good or evil. Although we may not appreciate that some black widow spiders kill their mates, we do not call black widow spiders immoral. We say it is the nature of the black widow to kill her mate. On the other hand, if a woman kills her mate, we call the action immoral. Therefore, morality can only exist in human beings.

James believed that moral philosophers such as the utilitarians had only a partial understanding of the meaning of good:

> Various essences of good have been . . . proposed as bases of the ethical system. . . .
>
> No one of the measures that have been actually proposed has, however given general satisfaction. . . . The best, on the whole, of these marks and measures of goodness seems to be the capacity to bring happiness. But in order not to break down fatally, this test must be taken to cover innumerable acts and impulses that never *aim* at happiness; so that, after all, in seeking for a universal principle,—that *the essence of good is simply to satisfy demand.* The demand may be for anything under the sun. There is really no more ground for supposing that all our demands can be accounted for by

one universal underlying kind of motive than there is ground for supposing that all physical phenomena are cases of a single law. [19]

James believed there are general moral principles that all people should act on, but there cannot be specific moral rules for every situation. For instance, there is a difference between the specific moral rule, "Never take a drink," and a general moral principle such as, "Act for the greatest good for the greatest number" of people. The first moral rule applies to a specific demand, while the latter one requires us to look more deeply into a general moral principle. General moral principles urge us to think carefully about our choices.

Religion

James had deep respect for a religion that enriches our lives, one that has cash-value, in his words. He noted that people in all cultures turn to an active god or gods who "gets things done." If people do not believe in God, James said, it may be because God is not active or not accomplishing things in these people's lives.

We have no absolute proof for God's existence, but for James, people who believe in God have a better chance to discover God than people who disbelieve. If we do not leave open the possibility of God, then we face the risk of losing any chance of discovering God. In his work *The Will to Believe*, he wrote that our belief in God's existence enriches our lives in a way that disbelief cannot.

The practical needs and experiences of religion seem to me sufficiently met by the belief that beyond man and in a fashion continuous with him there exists a larger power which is friendly to him and his ideals. All that the facts require is that the power shall be other and larger than our conscious selves.

God is the natural appellation, for us Christians at least, for the supreme reality, so I will call this higher part of the universe by the name of God. We and God have business with each other; and in opening ourselves to his influence our deepest destiny is fulfilled. [20]

The Heroic Life

James believed that life without struggle is dull, mediocre, and empty. We can approach life in two ways, he says. In a life without risks, we choose safety and security. The other kind of life is heroic: a life in which we choose danger, courage, and risk.

James did not suggest that we take needless, harmful risks to live a heroic life. Rather, he was talking about a "real fight" for something important, such as the struggle between good and evil. We need to fight evil. We might find evil in the form of prejudice, animal cruelty, or toxic dumping. When we do, we can ignore it, simply voice our objections, or actively do something about the evil. If we confront it, we may be taking risks. To James, however, we have at least fought for an important cause.

> For my own part, I do not know what the sweat and blood of this life mean, if they mean anything short of this. If this life be not a real fight, in which something is eternally gained for the universe by success, it is no better than a game of private theatricals from which we may withdraw at will. But it *feels* like a real fight—as if there were something really wild in the universe which we, with all our idealities and faithfulnesses, are needed

to redeem: and first of all to redeem our own hearts from atheisms and fears. [21]

According to James, struggle and effort are vital elements of the good life. He believed that getting involved is better than sitting back and drifting along. Living a heroic life means that we must struggle by facing obstacles and taking risks.

Religious Conversion

For James, religious conversion is an intense change of consciousness in our lives that results in a spiritual outlook. Religious conversion brings us happiness even though we still see the presence of evil in the world.

The outcome of conversion leads into two areas: (1) saintliness in our conduct, and (2) mysticism, or "seeing the truth in a special manner." According to James, saints have courage in their soul. They are pure, charitable, and wise. He called saints a magic gift to humankind. Unlike worldly people, saints show little interest in material things. Their magic is that of the soul and not of the physical objects. The mystic, too, has a spiritual gift. Mystics experience the unity of opposites and the kinship of all life, which, to James, is reality in its truest sense.

Religious Experience

Religion, said James, is our most important function in life. If we look deeply into our own experiences, we "find evidence for God's existence." Our inner experiences help us realize that the world we live in is part of a spiritual universe that gives the world value. When we unite with that higher spiritual universe through prayer or some kind of inner communion with God, the spiritual energy flows in and through us and affects the world. Religious faith, he said, gives us a new love of life, and in that love, we experience a higher and richer moral order.

JOHN DEWEY

According to scholars, William James's beautifully written book *Varieties of Religious Experience* owns a space on the bookshelves of every literary library. Yet, John Dewey probably influenced more people. His major expression of pragmatism was in the social, rather than individual realm, and his most influential works related to education, democracy, ethics, religion, and art. Dewey's accomplishments earned him respect and admiration throughout the world.

Dewey's Life

John Dewey (1859–1952) was born and grew up in Burlington, Vermont. His father was a successful grocer, and his mother was deeply involved in charitable affairs. After graduating from the University of Vermont, Dewey taught classics, algebra, and science at a high school in Pennsylvania. Two years later, he enrolled in the doctoral program at Johns Hopkins University in Baltimore.

After graduating with his Ph.D., Dewey taught philosophy at the University of Michigan. While there, he married Alice Chipman, with whom he had five children and adopted a sixth. While teaching at Michigan, he turned to pragmatism. In 1894, he accepted a position as chairperson of the Department of Philosophy, Psychology, and Pedagogy at the University of Chicago. While there, he got the chance to put theory into practice. Dewey opened an experimental school, where he encouraged parents to take an active role in their children's education. It was so successful that his view on educational theory, with its emphasis on "learning by doing," spread across the country. In 1904, Dewey moved to Columbia University in New York where he taught and wrote for the next 25 years. He frequently lectured on his theories of education in Japan, China, and the Soviet Union (present-day Russia).

Always interested in social causes, Dewey was one of the organizers of the American Association of University Professors

John Dewey was an American philosopher, educational reformer, and psychologist whose progressive ideas had worldwide impact. Dewey addressed education, domestic and international politics, and social issues, including women's suffrage, progressive education, and educators' rights.

and of the American Civil Liberties Union (ACLU). He died at age 92.

Instrumentalism

For William James, pragmatism meant helping people out of their conflicts: If it is true for me that God exists, then I should act on that feeling. Like James, Dewey was interested in "practical problems," but unlike James, he was more interested in the problems of society than with inner religious experiences. Dewey saw a deep need to reorganize our social and physical environment. He criticized the empiricists for thinking that our ideas refer to fixed things in nature, and he criticized the rationalists, such as Descartes, for considering nature one thing and the mind another.

Dewey called his version of pragmatism "instrumentalism" or "experimentalism." Agreeing with Darwin's theory of evolution, Dewey viewed human beings as biological organisms. Based on this notion of biological evolution, Dewey believed that human beings would evolve morally, thus creating a better society through improvements in education. His philosophy of instrumentalism, he said, was a bridge between science and ethics, claiming, "We must have both [scientific] knowledge and practice." The key to creating a better society, said Dewey, is to reorganize our social environment, especially education, through practical experimentation.

Human Nature and Habits

According to Dewey, before we can reorganize society, we need to understand human nature. He viewed all humans as having natural impulses that differ in various social situations. Impulses may be explosive or not, but whatever the impulse, if it reflects itself in the same way time after time, then it becomes a habit. Dewey found two types of habits: intelligence and routine. Intelligence is by far the superior habit because, by using intelligence, we can reflect and then make necessary adjustments to our environment.

The function of reflective thought is to transform a situation in which there is experienced obscurity, doubt, conflict, disturbance of some sort, into a situation that is clear, coherent, settled, harmonious. . . .

When a situation arises containing a difficulty or perplexity, the person who finds himself in it may take one of a number of courses. He may dodge it, dropping the activity that brought it about, turning to something else. He may indulge in a flight of fancy, imagining himself powerful or wealthy, or in some other way in possession of the means that would enable him to deal with the difficulty. Or, finally, he may face the situation. In this case, he begins to reflect.

The moment he begins to reflect, he begins of necessity to observe in order to take stock of conditions. . . . Until the habit of thinking is well formed, facing the situation to discover the facts requires an effort. For the mind tends to dislike what is unpleasant and so to sheer off from an adequate notice of that which is especially annoying.[22]

Much of our thinking, said Dewey, is careless and shows little reflection. Most of us do not understand the relationships that exist among impulses, habits, and intelligence.

The Importance of Education

According to Dewey, education is the only way we can remake society. Yet, educational practices are often based on a misunderstanding of human nature. At an early age, children learn to avoid "the shock of unpleasant disagreements" and to find the easy way out by conforming to society's customs:

Very early in life sets of mind are formed without attentive thought, and these sets persist and control the mature mind. The child learns to avoid the shock of unpleasant disagreement, to find the easy way out, to appear to conform to customs which are wholly mysterious to him in order to get his own way—that is to display some natural impulse without exciting the unfavorable notice of those in authority. Adults distrust the intelligence which a child has while making upon him demands for a kind of conduct that requires a high order of intelligence, if it is to be intelligent at all. The inconsistency is reconciled by instilling in him "moral" habits which have a maximum of emotional empressment and adamantine hold with a minimum of understanding. These habitudes . . . govern conscious later thought. They are usually deepest and most unget-at-able just where critical thought is most needed—in morals, religion and politics.[23]

If children are taught at an early age to avoid critical discussion of "morals, religion, and politics," said Dewey, they are cut off from their own ability to think rationally about such subjects.

Dewey's method was to test all ideas in the "educational laboratory" where students could challenge different ideas and evaluate the consequences. In that way, students would learn *not* to conform to conventional "bad habits."

"Life," said Dewey, "is too complex and changing to make a set list of rules." We must learn to make intelligent choices. We must learn to distinguish between "desire and the desirable." Desire is the starting point, and then, before making decisions, we must engage in intelligent critical inquiry. By acting pragmatically, we will realize that, if we are to enjoy things, we may have to sacrifice other things before making moral choices.

LINKS TO PROCESS PHILOSOPHY

Although James and Dewey were both pragmatists, they each contributed something different to contemporary thinking. By combining philosophy and psychology, James had a strong influence on the important French philosopher Henri Bergson and on existentialism, a philosophical movement that came to prominence after World War II.

As an educational reformer, Dewey's impact is still felt in America's classrooms. His thinking influenced English-born Alfred North Whitehead, who wanted his philosophy to perform a social function. Together, Bergson and Whitehead launched a new system of thought called "process philosophy."

4

PROCESS PHILOSOPHY
Bergson and Whitehead

*The great moral figures that have made their mark
on history join hands across the centuries, above
our human cities; they unite into a divine city,
which they bid us enter.*
— Henri Bergson

A NEW WORLDVIEW

For centuries, philosophers and scientists had accepted English physicist and astronomer Isaac Newton's theory that we lived in a mechanical world that could be understood by gathering observable, measurable evidence and subjecting it to principles of reasoning and logic. By the nineteenth century, however, a change in this worldview had begun as developments in the physical and biological sciences questioned Newton's mechanistic world order.

Based on English naturalist Charles Darwin's findings of natural selection, a new worldview began to take shape. Human beings were now viewed as part of the biological landscape, subject to the same law of natural selection as the rest of biological life. We held no special place in the whole scheme of things, and just like other species, we have changed through the ages and continue to change.

After studying Darwin, philosophers Henri Bergson and Alfred North Whitehead became enthusiasts of the theory of evolution by natural selection. Yet, they disagreed with Darwin that the life process is the result of random chance. Bergson and Whitehead could not accept the idea that evolution happens haphazardly. Bergson set out to show that a force or principle directs the course of evolution, and Whitehead believed that everything is connected with everything else. These philosophers wanted to show there is a unity in life and that everything is interrelated in the evolutionary process. To Bergson and Whitehead, no part of the world is static, nor can any part work totally on its own.

HENRI BERGSON

In light of the evidence provided by Darwin, Bergson accepted the theory of evolution by natural selection. Bergson, however, felt that this ever-changing life process must be directed in some way. For him, evolution could not be the result of hit-and-miss chance. There must be some force, or principle, that guides the course of the changes that take place in the process of natural selection. Evolution, he said, appears to be directed and have a purpose.

Bergson's philosophy is dualistic, meaning that the world contains two opposing tendencies: (1) the life force, or *élan vital*, and (2) matter's resistance against the life force. We humans, he said, understand matter through our intellect or reason, with which we measure things in the world. Through the intellect, we formulate systems of science and see things as separate units in space, like the pieces of a jigsaw puzzle. In contrast with the intellect is our faculty of intuition. Intuition gives us insight into the life force that directs all growth and change: It sees the whole picture, not just parts of the picture.

Bergson's Life

Henri Bergson (1859–1941) was born in Paris, France. His father was from Polish-Jewish ancestry, and his mother from an English- and Irish-Jewish background. His father, a musician and composer, was the head of the Geneva conservatory in Switzerland. Educated at Lycées secondary school in Paris, Bergson excelled in mathematics and letters. One of his schoolmates described him as honest, sensitive to other's feelings, and innocent, although slightly withdrawn or detached. He said that Bergson was more of an observer of the human parade than a participant.

In college, Bergson's main interests were philosophy, mathematics, and science. After graduation, he became professor of philosophy at the Angers Lycée for two years. His lectures were so popular that students from all disciplines came to listen.

At the age of 30, he accepted the job of philosophy professor at the College Rollin in Paris. The next year, he married Louise Neuberger, and they gave birth to a daughter, who grew up to become a talented painter. In 1900, Bergson became professor of philosophy at the College de France, a post he held until 1921 when ill health forced him to retire. He received many honors, including election to the French Academy and, in 1927, the Nobel Prize in Literature.

Three years after the start of World War I, the League of Nations sent Bergson to the United States to persuade President Woodrow Wilson to enter the war. In 1932, he published his last work, *Two Sources of Morality and Religion*, which brought him even greater fame. At the onset of World War II in 1939, France became a member of the Allied forces fighting against Nazi Germany. The following year, the Nazis condemned Bergson for being a Jew, but it was proposed that, because of his

international reputation, he be exempt from the Vichy government's anti-Semitic measures. (The Vichy government was set
up in 1940 following France's military defeat at the hand of the
Nazis. They collaborated with the Nazis in many of their anti-
Semitic policies.) Bergson, however, refused to be treated more
favorably than other Jews. He resigned his various honors, and
although he was now a frail old man, Bergson stood in line with
his fellow Jews to sign the registry books, a policy emplaced by
the Nazis as part of their anti-Semitic harassment. He died a
few days later, in January 1941.

Intellect and Intuition

The key to understanding Bergson's philosophy is his notion of intellect and intuition. With intellect, he says, we are
"placed outside the object." With intuition, however, "we enter into it." It is intuition that gives us a direct insight into the
nature of reality.

> Philosophers . . . agree in distinguishing two profoundly
> different ways of knowing a thing. The first implies that
> we move round the object [intellect]; the second, that
> we enter into it [intuition]. The first depends on the
> point of view at which we are placed and on the sym-
> bols by which we express ourselves. The second neither
> depends on a point of view nor relies on any symbol.
> The first kind of knowledge may be said to stop at the
> *relative;* the second, in those cases where it is possible,
> to attain the *absolute.*
>
> Consider, for example, the movement of an object
> in space. My perception of the motion will vary with
> the point of view, moving or stationary, from which I
> observe it. My expression of it will vary with the sys-
> tem of axes, or points of reference, to which I relate

it, that is, with the symbols by which I translate it.
For this double reason I call such motion *relative:* in
the one case, as in the other, I am placed outside the
object itself. But when I speak of an *absolute* movement, I am attributing to the moving object an inte-
rior and, so to speak, states of mind; I also imply that
I am in sympathy with those states, and that I insert
myself in them by an effort of imagination. . . . I shall
no longer grasp the movement from without, remain-
ing where I am, but from where it is, from within, as it
is in itself. I shall possess an absolute. [24]

Evolution

Bergson's *élan vital* is the life force that results in the process
of natural selection. It is a force that directs the tendency to
change. Using the human eye as an example, Bergson argued
that the process of natural selection would tend to work against,
rather than in favor of, the development of the eye.

> Let us assume, to begin with, the Darwinian theory of
> insensible [slight and gradual] variations, and suppose
> the occurrence of small differences due to chance, and
> continually accumulating. It must not be forgotten that
> all of the parts of an organism are necessarily coordi-
> nated. Whether the function be the effect of the organ
> or its cause, it matters little; one point is certain, the
> organ will be of no use and will not give selection a
> hold unless it functions. However the minute structure
> of the retina may develop, and however complicated
> it may become, such progress, instead of favoring vi-
> sion, will probably hinder it if the visual centers do not
> develop at the same time, as well as several parts of the
> visual organ itself. If the variations are accidental how

can they ever agree to arise in every part of the organ at the same time, in such a way that the organ will continue to perform its function? [25]

By using the development of the eye as an example, Bergson argued for a directing principle that guided the development of evolution. Thus, for Bergson, reality is in a constant state of change in which nothing is permanent. The *élan vital*, he says, is a "current of consciousness" that penetrated matter and gave rise to living bodies, determining the course of their evolution.

Rising from matter, life took different directions. Plants took one direction, insects another, and higher intelligence still another. As they evolved, these directions, or functions, became more perfect and increased in consciousness. With the appearance of humans came the "reason to be" of life on Earth.

Time and Duration

Most of us understand time in moments, breaking these moments into units of seconds, minutes, and hours. The way we experience time, said Bergson, is not what time really is. Time is duration: It endures. It is impossible to break time into moments or even into past, present, and future because we cannot know where or when one moment ends and another moment begins. We experience time as an ever present *now*. When we look at time through the eyes of science, we see merely frozen moments, like snapshots, taken of a constantly changing process. For this reason, the mind does not grasp reality as a continuous, indivisible process. Time, said Bergson, is a state of flux and cannot be understood scientifically.

Our intellect understands the snapshots, but it cannot grasp duration. Only intuition can understand time in duration. Duration is reality, so if we are to understand the nature of reality correctly, we must understand it in terms of duration. With

Henri Bergson believed that intuition, not analysis or intellect, reveals the real world to us. Intuition, he argued, is a direct experience of the continuous flow of reality without the use of intellectual concepts.

intuition, we also can understand the universality of mathematics, science, and human nature.

The *Élan Vital*

The essence of the *élan vital* is duration. The *élan vital* drives all organisms toward higher organization because it is the essence of all living beings and the creative power that flows through all things. Yet, because humans have both intellect and intuition, we understand the *élan vital* in two different ways.

With the intellect, we separate the *élan vital* process into distinct, static states. We divide and analyze the flow of existence, but because the intellect is limited, it lacks the ability to grasp reality, so it divides experience into static snapshots.

Intuition, however, knows that reality is continuous and not snapshots of separate parts. Intuition participates in duration itself. Where intellect analyzes, divides, and separates, intuition synthesizes, unifies, and enters into the flow of existence. Intuition gives us a unified vision of reality as it truly is.

Bergson argued that evolution is creative because the future is open. By that he meant that evolution has no final goal: Duration always endures and creates new evolutionary events. According to Bergson, this vital impetus is "supra-conscious," and we could call it God. God is pure activity limited by the material world in which he struggles to manifest himself. God is constantly changing; therefore, he is neither all-powerful nor all-knowing. God is love and the object of love. Evolution is God creating creators, that he may have beings worthy of his love.

Morality and Religion

Bergson carried his theory of intellect and intuition into the fields of morality and religion. These sources of morality and religion are intellect and intuition. Bergson labeled his two moralities "closed morality" and "open morality." He labeled his two types of religion "static religion" and "dynamic religion."

Closed Morality

Bergson saw in human beings a basic instinct to form society. This social instinct ensures the survival and growth of civilization. In nature, bees and ants have instincts to form the hive and the hill, and they cannot vary from that instinct. We humans have an instinct to form society, yet, we also have reason or intellect to decide which type of society we want. Our social instinct, combined with the intellect's need to organize, is the basis of Bergson's closed morality.

The main concern of the closed morality is the good of the group, so we must develop customs and laws that provide a stable society. In a closed society, the individual is less important than concern for the society as a whole.

> Social life is thus immanent [within the limits of experience or knowledge], like a vague ideal, in instinct as well as in intelligence: this ideal finds its most complete expression in the hive or the ant-hill on the one hand, in human societies on the other. Whether human or animal, a society is an organization; it implies a co-ordination and generally also a subordination of elements; it therefore exhibits, whether merely embodied in life or, in addition, specifically formulated, a collection of rules and laws. . . .
>
> In human society we delve down to the root of the various obligations to reach obligation in general, the more obligation will tend to become necessity, the nearer it will draw, in its peremptory aspect, to instinct. [26]

Another characteristic of the closed morality is an attitude of *exclusivity*. Because the closed morality is a morality for the good of the group, it necessarily excludes those individuals who do not belong. The attitude of exclusivity creates a sense of belonging to one's group, and at the same time, views those outside the group as a threat.

Exclusivity means that we support the values of our group but not of groups that have different values. There is *our* way and the *wrong* way. For example, if we find the values of another nation threatening to our values, we may go to war with them to protect our society. However, within our society, we also have exclusivity. We see it in sports: Our team is more important than your team. We see exclusivity in politics: Our party is best for the country, your party will ruin the country. We also see exclusivity in religion: Our religion has the truth, yours is false. In closed morality, exclusivity is necessary for the survival of the group. It gives us security and a sense of belonging.

If we look at ourselves honestly, Bergson claimed, we see that the closed morality is a fundamental part of our nature. It appears to be part of our biological heritage. It has provided for our continued survival and is a part of ourselves that we cannot deny.

Open Morality

Just as closed morality depends upon an intellectual view of reality that analyzes and divides, open morality relies on the intuition of unity in nature. Through intuition, reality is directly experienced as a continuous process. This intuitive ability allows the individual to understand reality and humanity in a universal way. The ideal goal of the open morality is a condition in which all human beings are free to develop and to realize their creative capacities. The goal of open morality is that all human beings should live fuller, more active, more conscious, and more spontaneous lives.

Whereas the closed morality is exclusive, the open morality is *inclusive*. It is a morality for all humankind and not the good of just one society. The social order of this morality is an ideal open society that welcomes all human beings.

The open morality focuses on the creative self-realization of the individual. From Socrates to the present, we have heard the cry of moral heroes proclaiming, "To your own self be true." Bergson looked to such mystics as Jesus, Buddha, and the saints of all the world's religions as the true moral heroes. They draw us toward an ideal society that includes everyone.

Bergson said that open morality and closed morality are within each of us and that this moral duality is the source of our inner moral conflict. Alongside our capacity for prejudice toward others exists our capacity for universal love. Alongside our deep sense of national pride is the awareness that all people are worthy of respect.

Static and Dynamic Religion

Bergson believed that this moral duality expresses itself in two types of religion: static religion and dynamic religion. Static religion has its roots in the closed morality. The primary focus of static religion is on ritual and doctrine. Static religions have a set of dogmas that belong exclusively to a particular religious denomination. Thus, static religion expresses the same attitude of exclusivity that we find in closed morality. Those who do not follow the rules of dogma, ritual, and basic doctrine are excluded from the group.

Dynamic religion, however, shows little concern with accepting dogma or participating in ritual. Bergson saw dynamic religion, like open morality, represented in the lives of the great moral teachers throughout history such as Moses, Socrates, Buddha, Lao Tzu, Jesus, Muhammad, and others. These teachers were examples of the finished products of the evolutionary process. They represent a possibility for all of us, and it is entirely up to us to choose to fulfill our destiny or to choose not to fulfill our destiny.

> Mankind lies groaning, half crushed beneath the weight of its own progress. Men do not sufficiently realize that their future is in their own hands. Theirs is the task of determining first of all whether they want to go on living

or not. Theirs is the responsibility, then, for deciding if they want merely to live, or intend to make just the extra effort required for fulfilling, even on their refractory planet, the essential function of the universe, which is a machine for the making of gods. [27]

ALFRED NORTH WHITEHEAD

Alfred North Whitehead was another philosopher who saw everything in the world united in process. Like Thomas Dewey, Whitehead wanted his philosophy to perform a social function, to make human life richer and more significant. Dewey saw his task in terms of solving a variety of immediate problems, such as education, but Whitehead took a different view. He regarded philosophy as more a matter of understanding the world than of changing it.

Whitehead's main theme was that everything is connected. What science tends to separate, philosophy must try to see as an organic unity. According to Whitehead, "the red glow of the sunset should be as much a part of nature as are the molecules and electric waves." In other words, he hoped to show the interrelationship among the various elements of science and nature. Although he shared these same concerns with Bergson, Whitehead explored metaphysics in a whole new way.

Whitehead's Life

Alfred North Whitehead (1861–1947) was born in Ramsgate, Kent, in southern England. His father, a pastor in the Church of England, educated his son at home. When Alfred was 14, his parents enrolled him in Sherborne School where he received a classical education. A brilliant student, Whitehead received a scholarship to study mathematics at Trinity College, Cambridge. After graduation, he taught mathematics at Trinity for the next 25 years.

While teaching at Trinity, Whitehead married Evelyn Wade, and they had four children. During his teaching career at Trinity, Bertrand Russell enrolled as Whitehead's student, and the two men became lifelong friends. Later, he and Russell, who was to become an influential philosopher and mathematician, collaborated on their famous work on mathematical logic and philosophy, *Principia Mathematica*.

From Trinity College, Whitehead moved to London. At first, he had no job, so he washed bottles, but soon, the University of London hired him as professor of mathematics. He became the dean of the faculty of science and president of the university's senate. There, he developed an interest in the problems of higher education, especially with the impact of modern industrial civilization upon student learning. Through the years, he had been writing major works, but now Whitehead's efforts turned to his theory of "connectedness."

At age 63, Whitehead came to the United States to accept a position in the philosophy department at Harvard University. He taught at Harvard for the next 13 years. Each week, he and his wife held open house for students, providing hot chocolate and lots of good conversation. During his years at Harvard, Whitehead produced his most influential philosophical works, *Science and the Modern World, Adventure of Ideas,* and *Process and Reality.* At age 77, Whitehead retired. He died ten years later, in 1947.

The Purpose of Philosophy

Like Bergson, Whitehead wanted to replace static scientific views with dynamic, active views. Philosophy's purpose, he said, is to search for the underlying pattern in the universe.

The use of philosophy is to maintain an active novelty of fundamental ideas illuminating the social system. It

Alfred North Whitehead made critical contributions to mathematics, logic, the philosophy of science, and the study of metaphysics. He offered a concept of God as being interdependent with the world yet developing with it, rejecting the idea of a perfect and all-powerful God.

reverses the slow descent of accepted thought towards the inactive commonplace. If you like to phrase it so, philosophy is mystical. For mysticism is direct insight

into depths as yet unspoken. But the purpose of philosophy is to rationalize mysticism: not by explaining it
away, but by the introduction of novel verbal character-
izations, rationally coordinated.

Philosophy is akin to poetry, and both of them seek
to express that ultimate good sense which we term civilization. In each case there is reference to form beyond
the direct meanings of words. Poetry allies itself to me-
tre, philosophy to mathematical pattern. [28]

For Whitehead, only a "process philosophy" could account
for the creativity and interdependence of our experience. It is
not the business of philosophy to analyze the world logically, he
said, because such analysis separates the world into pieces. Philosophy, like mysticism and poetry, should explore the depths
and then try to explain those depths in a rational way.

Because we are finite, it is not possible for us to understand
the infinite. Yet, insisted Whitehead, if we look closely, we find
a pattern that shows that the ultimate nature of all things is in
harmony. Everything is interconnected, and the universe is rational. We can find the pattern in mathematics, which is the
tool for our insights into all connections.

The science of Pure Mathematics, in its modern developments, may claim to be the most original creation
of the human spirit. . . . [Its] originality consists in the
fact that in mathematical science connections between
things are exhibited, which, apart from the agency of
human reason, are extremely unobvious.[29]

The Universe as Process

Whitehead disagreed with early Greek philosophers and Isaac
Newton who held that atoms are located in space and time and

are therefore isolated from each other. If this were true, the universe would be mechanical, and we would be able to study each element as separate from other elements. The universe, however, is not mechanical, and it is not static. For Whitehead, nothing is isolated. Instead, everything is interrelated and in "process." No element in the world is ever isolated, because nature is a living organism. *Everything* in the universe contains the principle of life.

Whitehead claimed that the process theory frees us from Descartes's dualism and the mind-body problem, which argued that the mind is separate from the body. Everything, Whitehead said, exists in relation to something else, and everything is in a state of flux and interconnected. Although every experience we have affects us, no two experiences are exactly the same. We cannot even think the same way twice because each experience changes us, and, therefore, after each experience we are different. This is true not only for all human beings but also for all nature.

Part of the process of change is death. For Whitehead, death is only the creativity of the universe moving on to the next birth. Everything in the world comes into being, takes on a form or character, and dies. Then other new entities come into being. Yet, the unique character of each entity continues in the flow of the process like memory preserved through time.

Because everything is in the process of evolving, nothing can be totally understood because it is always changing. According to Whitehead, the only permanence in the world is in the realm of possibility, and these possibilities are eternal objects: "The problem of evolution is the development of enduring harmonies of enduring shapes of value, which merge into higher attainments of things beyond themselves." [30]

God

To call eternal objects "possibilities" required that Whitehead answer how these possibilities exist and how they are relevant. To answer this question, he said there is a timeless entity, and that is God. This God is not a creator god. This God is creative. God is "not *before* all creation, but *with* all creation," Whitehead said.

> We require God as the Principle of Concretion. This position can be substantiated only by the discussion of the general implication . . . of the process of realization.
>
> We conceive actuality as in essential relation to an unfathomable possibility. Eternal objects inform actual occasions with hierarchic patterns, included and ex-cluded in every variety of discrimination. Another view of the same truth is that every actual occasion is a limi-tation imposed on possibility, and that by virtue of this limitation the particular value of that shaped together-ness of things emerges. . . .
>
> God is the ultimate limitation, for just that limita-tion which it stands in His nature to impose. God is not concrete, but He is the ground for concrete actuality. No reason can be given for the nature of God, because that nature is the ground of rationality. . . .
>
> We have come to the limit of rationality. . . . What further can be known about God must be sought in the region of particular experiences, and therefore rests on an empirical basis. In respect to the interpretation of these experiences mankind have differed profoundly. He has been named respectively, Jehovah, Allah, Brahma, Father in Heaven, Order of Heaven, First Cause, Su-preme Being, Chance. Each name corresponds to a sys-tem of thought derived from the experiences of those who have used it. [31]

Through creativity, God brings into existence entities and events. God's nature is consciousness and eternal goodness.

Whitehead argued that our conceptual feelings come from God's nature and are realized through the expression of his role as goodness and conscious activity.

According to Whitehead, the creative process is orderly because of eternal objects, or possibilities, and these possibilities exist in God, as his nature. God mediates between the eternal objects and this world and chooses the appropriate possibilities from the realm of eternal objects. When humans choose God's possibilities, we have order and harmony, but when we reject them, the result is discord and evil. Thus, evil is not the result of God's will, but it exists despite his purpose to abolish it. It is up to humankind to help in this "increasingly successful, though still imperfect," process of gaining victory over evil.

LINKS TO ANALYTIC PHILOSOPHY

The philosophies of Bergson and Whitehead planted seeds for twentieth-century quantum physics and alternative views in philosophy. Bergson thought that we could not find the answers to the important "why" questions in any of the earlier philosophical traditions of rationalism. He believed the ability to know why things evolve and change could only be found through intuition. As a metaphysician, Whitehead saw the universe in process and saw philosophical thinking as open-ended. Mathematicians were impressed by the boldness of his thought.

The philosophers who followed Bergson and Whitehead, however, rejected the thinking of process philosophy. These "analytic" philosophers, as they are called, were antimetaphysicians. They showed little or no interest in process philosophy or in any traditional philosophy to date. These philosophers wrote only for other philosophers and not for the intelligent public. For them, the task of philosophy was to clarify our thoughts through an analysis of language. The problems of philosophy, they said, revolve around the meanings and usages of language.

5

ANALYTIC PHILOSOPHY
Russell, Logical Positivism, and Wittgenstein

*The limits of my language are
the limits of my reality.*
—Ludwig Wittgenstein

ANALYTIC PHILOSOPHY

Throughout the ages, philosophers have asked difficult, probing questions such as, "Who am I?" "Does life have meaning?" "Where does the world come from?" "How much can we know?" "What is reality?" "How should we act?" "Is there a God?" The answers that were developed laid the foundations for the great systems of Western philosophy. Yet, a movement arose in the Western world known as analytic philosophy that rejected these vast systems of thought. Analytic philosophers looked with scorn on philosophies that told people how they should behave, or even worse, what human nature is. For the analytic thinkers, the only task of philosophy is to clarify the meaning of language. They refused to speculate on reality, the universe, or the meaning of life because they held that no one should try to explain what language could not clarify.

The task of philosophy, they argued, is to "unpack" complex problems arising from the unclear use of language, including that used by scientists. The analytic philosophers wanted to clarify such scientific terminology by "rigorous linguistic analysis." In this way, they hoped to get rid of what they considered fuzzy thinking.

BERTRAND RUSSELL

English analytic philosopher Bertrand Russell wanted to analyze facts for the purpose of inventing a new language called "logical atomism." This new language would possess the exactness and clarity of mathematics because it would correspond exactly to the facts. Russell emphasized that philosophy is not concerned with discovery but with clarification. He had little interest in truth as such, but he did have a deep interest in the meaning of language.

For Russell, logic should form the basis of language because through logic one could accurately express everything that could be clearly stated. Through his logical atomism, he sought to develop a language that corresponded to objects in the world; he wanted to make sure that every statement represented an adequate picture of the world of facts. Unlike Bergson and Whitehead, who viewed everything in the world as interconnected, Russell held that the world is a collection of wholly independent entities that could be analyzed. If we use William James's classification of temperaments, we would call Russell and other analytic philosophers tough-minded rather than tender-minded.

Russell's Life

Bertrand Russell (1872–1970) was born in Wales to a distinguished aristocratic English family. His father and mother were Lord and Lady Amberley. His godfather was the utilitarian philosopher John Stuart Mill. When Russell was only two years old, his father died. His mother died the following year. Bertrand and his brother were sent to live with their paternal grandfather,

Lord John Russell, who was 85 years old. When Bertrand was six years old, his grandfather died.

His grandmother, a countess and strict Protestant, refused to send the boys to boarding school. Instead, she hired governesses and tutors to educate them at home. Alone much of the time, Russell was unhappy, and during his teenage years, he often thought of committing suicide. The only thing that kept him alive was his love for mathematics. During his teen years, he had an intuition that God did not exist. This experience gave him great relief from his grandmother's rigid religious views.

When he was 18, Russell went to Cambridge University to study mathematics and philosophy. His undergraduate years were the happiest period of his life because for the first time he had friends his own age. While at Cambridge as a fellow and lecturer, Russell wrote several important works in philosophy and mathematics, including *Principia Mathematics* with Alfred North Whitehead. In 1916, the university dismissed him for his pacifist activities during World War I. While serving a six-month term in prison for his activities, he continued to write important philosophical and mathematical books and many papers.

Russell was a strong believer in education, which he thought could help rid a person of their prejudices. In 1927, he and his wife, Dora, founded the experimental Beacon Hill School in England. In 1931, his brother died, and Bertrand Russell became the third earl of Russell. When Parliament debarred him for his lack of religious beliefs, he went to the United States where he taught at the University of Chicago, the University of California at Los Angeles (UCLA), and then, in 1940, at City College in New York.

In 1930, Russell had written a popular book, *Marriage and Morals,* and because of his liberal attitude in the book toward sexual morals, City College dismissed him from his position, claiming he was "morally unfit" to teach. He joined the Barnes Foundation, a museum and art school in Philadelphia, lecturing on philosophy, and then, in 1944, he returned to Cambridge University as a lecturer.

In 1961, he again landed in prison, this time for participating in demonstrations against nuclear weapons—although he had given up his pacifistic thinking at the outset of Nazi aggression in World War II, years earlier. In 1967, he organized a war crimes tribunal to hold America responsible for the war in Vietnam. Although he spent much of his life working to make the world a better place, he wrote, "The secret of happiness is to face the fact that the world is horrible."

Russell received many honors in his life. Among them was the British Order of Merit, a reward for distinguished service in science, art, literature, or the promotion of culture. In 1967, he received the prestigious Nobel Prize in Literature. He said that three passions had governed his life: the longing for love, the search for knowledge, and an unbearable pity for the suffering of humankind. Russell died in 1970 at age 99.

Logical Atomism

For Russell, logic is the essence of philosophy and the foundation of mathematics. In their *Principia Mathematica*, Russell and Whitehead wanted to construct a logic in which all mathematics could be derived from a few logical axioms. For example, let the symbols p and q stand for any two propositions so that we can say, "If p is true, then p or q is true." (An example of this would be to let the symbol p stand for the statement "if it rains," and then let q stand for the statement "the streets get wet.") Based on these findings, Russell thought that logic also could form the basis of a language that would accurately express everything that was clearly stated. Thus, specifically

Bertrand Russell was a philosopher, essayist, and social critic best known for his work in analytic philosophy and mathematical logic. His most important contributions were his theories of definite descriptions and logical atomism, in which he argued that the focus of philosophy should not be on discovery but rather on clarification.

constructed logical language would correspond to the world and be more precise and clear than the language we normally speak. It would be a "logically perfect language" without any misleading vagueness.

In a logically perfect language, there will be one word
and no more for every simple object, and everything
that is not simple will be expressed by a combination
of words, by a combination derived, of course, from the
words for the simple things that enter in, one word for
each simple component. A language of that sort will be
completely analytic, and will show at a glance the logical structure of the facts asserted or denied. [32]

Russell thought that our ordinary talk leads us away from
the logic of philosophical problems. Therefore, to create a new
language, he decided to analyze the difference between facts
and things. In the world, things have a variety of properties and
are in a variety of relations to each other. "That they have these
properties and relations are facts," said Russell. Facts make up
the complex relations of things to each other, and because they
are complex, facts are subject to analysis. Logical analysis aims
to make sure that language statements accurately represent the
facts of the world.

For Russell, in a logically perfect language, there should be
definite descriptions. A definite description takes the form of
"the so and so." Sentences with this type of form can be para-
doxical. Consider the statement, "The golden mountain does
not exist." Although this may appear as a true statement, Russell asked us to analyze it logically. How can it be true that the
golden mountain does not exist unless the phrase "the golden
mountain" is meaningful? We have to ask, "*What* does not exist?" That question implies that the "golden mountain" must
have some sort of reality or we could not say it does not exist.
Is it true, then, that "the golden mountain" does not mean anything? Russell set out to solve this puzzle.

Russell explained that it is a mistake to think of the phrase
"the golden mountain" as a name like Socrates or the Nile

River. Logically, we can see that "the golden mountain" is not an exact description or a name. Logically, we can say, "There exists no thing which is both golden and a mountain." The clearness of this statement leaves no question in our minds. Thus, we solve the puzzle by increasing clarity of thought.

For Russell, an atomic statement, or simple fact, is either true or false. We shall call a true statement *"p,"* and a false statement we shall call *"not-p."* Molecular statements consist of two or more atomic statements. For example, *p* and *q* can be linked together with such logical connectives as *and* or *or*. A statement such as *p* symbolizes "the dog has black spots" and *q* symbolizes "the dog is a male" is true only if the statements *p* and *q* are each true. No atomic fact corresponds to the entire statement, so we can only determine the truth or falsity of each of its statements. By adding more numbers to *p* and *q*, we can state more statements symbolically. Thus, logical analysis increases clarity of thought.

Moral Philosophy

For Russell, ethics, or morality, is merely personal, and because it has nothing to do with logic or facts, it has no place in philosophy.

> If we assert that this or that has "value," we are giving expression to our own emotions, not to a fact which would still be true if our personal feelings were different. To make this clear, we must try to analyze the conception of the Good. . . .
>
> When a man says "this is good in itself," he *seems* to be making a statement, just as much as if he said "this is square" or "this is sweet." I believe this to be a mistake. I think that what the man really means is: "I wish everybody to desire this," or rather "Would that everybody

desired this." If what he says is interpreted as a statement, it is merely an affirmation of his own personal
wish; if, on the other hand, it is interpreted in a general
way, it states nothing, but merely desires something.
The wish, as an occurrence, is personal, but what it desires is universal. It is, I think, this curious interlocking
of the particular and the universal which has caused so
much confusion in ethics. [33]

According to Russell, morality is merely personal. If you desire something, then that desire is good. Our notion of good is
nothing more than our personal desire. On a larger scale, the
good of society is the desire of society.

Nature, said Russell, has no morality, but we humans desire to create morals, and that is how ethics arise. Yet, not all
humans agree on what is good or bad. For example, the Aztecs
ate their enemies captured in war. We say eating people is bad.
In the United States, we disagree on such moral issues as abortion, euthanasia, and capital punishment. Because of these differences of opinion, said Russell, morality is obviously personal
desire and has nothing to do with universal truths.

Sex

Russell's liberal attitude toward morals included sexual practices. As mentioned earlier, because of his views on sexual relations, City College of New York canceled his appointment
in 1940. Below is a passage about sex from his popular work
Marriage and Morals.

If sex is not to be an obsession, it should be regarded by
the moralists as food has come to be regarded. . . . Sex
is a natural human need like food and drink. It is true
that men can survive without it, whereas they cannot

survive without food and drink, but from a psychological standpoint the desire for sex is precisely analogous to the desire for food and drink. . . . Healthy, outward-looking men and women are not to be produced by the thwarting of natural impulse, but by the equal and balanced development of all the impulses essential to a happy life. [34]

Education

Russell held a strong interest in education, but he questioned passive acceptance of the teacher's knowledge.

Passive acceptance of the teacher's wisdom is easy to most boys and girls. It involves no effort of independent thought, and seems rational because the teacher knows more than his pupils; it is moreover the way to win the favour of the teacher unless he is a very exceptional man. Yet the habit of passive acceptance is a disastrous one in later life. It causes men to seek a leader, and to accept as a leader whoever is established in that position.[35]

LOGICAL POSITIVISM

In 1922, Moritz Schlick was a professor of philosophy at the University of Vienna in Austria. That same year, Schlick and a group of Viennese intellectuals that included mathematicians, physicists, sociologists, and economists began to meet periodically for discussions. Like Russell, they wanted to show that metaphysics is impossible. They set out to do this by developing a new logic to prove that our knowledge is limited to sense experience. This group called themselves "logical positivists."

Refusing to speculate on anything metaphysical, which meant everything otherworldly or supernatural, the logical positivists relied entirely on the verification principle. The verification principle rejects anything that cannot be verified, or proved. Verification always rests on empirical observation in sense experience.

If we want to understand a statement, we must first have evidence of its truth. The method used for verification is observation. If we want to verify that "the cat is on the mat," then we must look at the mat and see the cat on it. Philosopher Rudolph Carnap, a member of the Vienna Circle, wanted to call this thinking the "logic of science." The task of the logic of science, he said, was to construct an artificial language in which every symbol referred to a concept and was verifiable. As it turned out, the verification principle needed verification itself. After realizing this, the logical positivists relented slightly on their total rejection of metaphysics.

Although the logical positivists struggled to make philosophy the logic of science, the Vienna Circle gradually broke up. First, in 1936, a mentally disturbed student murdered Schlick for refusing to approve the student's dissertation. In 1938, when Nazi Germany annexed Austria, the Vienna Circle dissolved. Some members of the group immigrated to the United States and others to England.

Although logical positivism had an enormous impact, its lifespan was short-lived. The logical positivists tried to develop an ideal language whose structure would exactly mirror the world. In the end, it did not work, although their no-nonsense, tough-minded point of view was useful to the advancement of knowing what will or will not work philosophically.

LUDWIG WITTGENSTEIN

Ludwig Wittgenstein wanted to bring an end to philosophy, and he thought that he had accomplished his task twice. Between the time of publication of his *Tractatus Logico-Philosophicus* (1919) and his *Philosophical Investigations* (1953), published after his death, Wittgenstein had a change of heart, the older man disowning the work of the younger one. Yet, the older man and the younger man agreed that language gives a picture of the world, and, in Wittgenstein's words, "The limits of my language are the limits of my reality."

Though both of Wittgenstein's books deal with language and meaning, in his later work, he moved away from Russell and the logical positivists and stepped closer to Nietzsche. Yet, there were vast differences in their approaches because Nietzsche was literary while Wittgenstein's writing was empirical and tough-minded.

Wittgenstein's Life

Ludwig Wittgenstein (1899–1951), the youngest of eight children, was born to a wealthy family in Vienna. His father was an engineer and industrialist, and his mother was a talented musician. Composer Johannes Brahms was a close friend of the family's and made frequent visits. All of his siblings had both artistic and intellectual talent, but they were each emotionally unstable. Three of his four brothers committed suicide. Ludwig himself considered suicide and fought emotional instability much of his life. His other brother lost a hand in World War I, but he went on to become a concert pianist. Persistence, an obvious trait of his pianist brother, was also one of Ludwig's major characteristics.

Until he was 14, Wittgenstein was educated at home, but he was more interested in tinkering with machinery than studying. Finally, his parents sent him to school at Linz, Austria, to learn mathematics and the physical sciences. After three years at Linz, he decided to study engineering. While he was an engineering student, he invented a propeller. In 1911, he became so intrigued with Bertrand Russell's *Principles of Mathematics* that he gave up engineering to study with Russell at Cambridge.

Under Russell's guidance, Wittgenstein launched into philosophy, especially logic. His aim was to solve all the traditional philosophical problems, and, in his first work, he claimed to have done just that. He said that, like his father, he was a businessman, and he was doing away with the business of philosophy. He dedicated his *Tractatus*, the work that so strongly influenced the logical positivists, to his friend and fellow student David Pinsent. He and Pinsent did experiments with rhythm in music. Wittgenstein would whistle or play the clarinet while Pinsent accompanied him on the piano. Wittgenstein's philosophical writings have many allusions to music.

Pinsent affirmed that Wittgenstein often thought of suicide "as a possibility," but studying logic with Russell was his salvation. In 1913, Wittgenstein went to Norway to write. There, he built a hut near the sea and lived like a hermit for two years with the seagulls as his only companions.

When World War I broke out, Wittgenstein volunteered in the Austrian Army. He rejected a commission and fought as an ordinary soldier, winning medals for bravery. He spent nearly a year as a prisoner of war in an Italian war camp, where he finished writing his first major work of philosophy.

Wittgenstein received a large fortune from his father's inheritance but gave the fortune to his sisters and became an elementary school teacher. Unsuited for teaching young children, he left to work as a gardener in a monastery. To take Wittgenstein's mind off committing suicide, his sister asked him to build her a large house in Vienna. He agreed, but his obsession with perfection nearly drove the workers crazy.

In 1929, he returned to Cambridge, received his doctorate in philosophy, and accepted a position as lecturer. While giving

Ludwig Wittgenstein contributed numerous original ideas to logic and the philosophies of mathematics, language, and mind. He boldly claimed that his major work, *Tractatus Logico-Philosophicus*, had solved all the major problems of philosophy by clearly explaining the logic of language.

lectures, he would recline in a deck chair—and told his students to bring their own. After class, he would rush off to the movies and watch any film, trying to forget "the futility of his profession." He especially liked watching cowboy films.

When World War II broke out, Wittgenstein volunteered as a medical orderly, believing that simple work was virtuous. In 1944, he returned to his Cambridge position but was unhappy with his teaching, so he resigned to finish his second major work, *Philosophical Investigations.* He went first to the Irish countryside near Dublin and then to a cottage on the west coast of Ireland. Although his health was not good, he went to the United States to spend some time with a friend. When he returned to England, he was diagnosed with cancer. Having no wish to live, and realizing he would soon die, he worked hard to finish *Investigations*, which was published two years after his death. When the doctor told Wittgenstein that the end was near, he said, "Good!" Two days later, he died.

The *Tractatus*

The most important task for Wittgenstein was the need to be clear about the logic of our language. Only then can we understand the limits of language. For example, philosopher Immanuel Kant had said that we can think of the noumenal world (the world of God, freedom, and immortality), but because our knowledge is limited to our experience of this world, we cannot know with certainty the noumenal world. Wittgenstein was more radical than Kant because he set a limit to both knowledge and thinking. Wittgenstein argued that Kant's noumenal world is not even *thinkable*. To even try to think about it is nonsense, and to try to talk about it is like saying, "It is unsayable, but let's talk about it anyway." In the preface of his book the *Tractatus*, Wittgenstein wrote:

The book deals with the problems of philosophy, and shows, I believe, that the reason why these problems are posed is that the logic of our language is misunderstood. The whole sense of the book might be summed up in the following words: what can be said at all can be said clearly, and what we cannot talk about we must pass over in silence.

Thus the aim of this book is to set a limit to thought, or rather—not to thought, but to the expression of thoughts: for in order to be able to set a limit to thought, we should have to find both sides of the limit thinkable (i.e., we should have to be able to think what cannot be thought).

It will therefore only be in language that the limit can be set, and what lies on the other side of the limit will simply be nonsense. [36]

Picturing

For Wittgenstein, the structure of language must somehow give us a "picture" of the world. The picture may correctly or incorrectly represent the facts, but without pictures there would be no representation at all. Wittgenstein gave the example of an automobile accident being reenacted by lawyers, using dolls and toy cars to represent real people and real automobiles involved in the accident. The picture portrayed by the lawyers represents what might have been the facts. Although the lawyers probably present conflicting pictures of the accident, without the pictures there would be no representation.

It is impossible to tell from a picture alone whether the events of the accident are true or false. So, no matter how closely you inspect the picture of the accident, you cannot tell if it represents the accident correctly. To tell if a picture is true, you have to be sure it fits the facts. Thus, you can never tell before you know the facts whether a picture is true.

The Mystical

The logical positivists liked Wittgenstein's idea that most philosophy is nonsense. The only useful method in philosophy, said Wittgenstein, would be to say only what can be said through observing facts—and this has little to do with philosophy. This outlook made Wittgenstein as tough-minded as the other logical positivists. Yet, Wittgenstein made other statements that upset the positivists by admitting that his own philosophical statements were nonsense. Recall that he wrote in *Tractatus*, "What can be said at all can be said clearly and what we cannot speak about we must pass over in silence." Such a statement was way too much like mysticism for the logical positivists to accept. They worried that Wittgenstein might find some important meaning in this silence.

For Wittgenstein, there *are* "things" we cannot put into words. These include our religious experiences and our moral values. These things are not facts because we cannot prove them. Still, even to mention such things left Russell and the logical positivists feeling uneasy. At this point, however, Wittgenstein dropped out of philosophy. He sought solitude, tried teaching elementary school, and then went to the United States. During his absence from writing philosophy, he began to think that language was not as limited as he had previously thought. With this in mind, he started to work on his new ideas, the ones we find in *Philosophical Investigations.*

THE "NEW" WITTGENSTEIN

In the *Tractatus,* Wittgenstein had written that the only function of language is to state facts and that the structure of language is logical and is the picture of the world. By a picture of language, he meant giving names to objects, shapes, colors, pains, moods, and numbers. Naming, he said, is like attaching a label to something. Now, however, he decided that language functions in a context, and many contexts and many meanings are possible.

Philosophers have always used names as the key to meaning. Plato argued that words were names of Forms, unchanging nonmaterial essences in the intelligible world. The physical world was merely the appearance of the world of Forms. Aristotle agreed that words named something unchanging, but he saw the unchanging in the world; namely, in substances.

The empiricists had argued that words named only what we experience with our senses. The pragmatists believed that words named actions. The logical positivists, Russell, and the early Wittgenstein thought that words named facts. The "new" Wittgenstein, however, discovered that the meaning of a word is its *use.* Like the tools in a toolbox that serve different functions, the word is a "tool" that can serve many functions.

> Think of the tools in a tool-box: there is a hammer, pliers, a saw, a screw-driver, a rule, a glue-pot, nails and screws.—The functions of words are as diverse as the functions of these objects. (And in both cases there are similarities.)
>
> Of course, what confuses us is the uniform appearance of words when we hear them spoken or meet them in script and print. For their *application* is not presented to us so clearly. Especially not, when we are doing philosophy.
>
> It is like looking into the cabin of a locomotive. We see handles all looking alike. (Naturally, since they are all supposed to be "handled.") But one is the handle of a crank which can be moved continuously (it regulates the opening of a valve); another is the handle of a switch, which has only two effective positions, it is either off or on; a third is the handle of a brake-lever, the harder one pulls on it, the harder it brakes; a forth, the handle of a pump: it has an effect only so long as it is moved to and fro. [37]

For the new Wittgenstein, the meaning of language is how well it gets the job done. For example, most of us say, "The Sun is coming up," or, "The Sun is setting," although science teaches us that the Sun neither rises nor sets. The appearance of a setting Sun is caused by Earth turning on its axis as it revolves around the Sun. As we watch the Sun set, we do not say, "Earth is turning on its axis." Such an explanation may be factual, but it is not useful: It does not get the job done.

Words do not just name objects. They also give substance to exclamations such as "Away! Ow! Help! Fine! No!" Language, Wittgenstein discovered, is like a game.

Language Games

How is language like a game? Both have rules. All games have rules that must be followed for the game to be played properly and enjoyed. Language games also have rules: rules of grammar, syntax, and semantics. If we do not follow the rules, language loses its meaning.

Sometimes, said Wittgenstein, when we use a word such as *God*, language "takes a holiday." Different religions explain the word *God* in different ways. Which way is correct? Broken language rules, he said, can result in a certain kind of madness. He gave Lewis Carroll's *Alice in Wonderland,* one of his favorite books, as an example. The White King asks Alice if she sees anyone down the road. "I see nobody on the road," says Alice. The King replies, "I only wish I had such eyes to be able to see Nobody! And at that distance, too!" Wittgenstein used this example to show us that logical analysis cannot discover the meaning of language.

The Role of Philosophy

For the new Wittgenstein, the role of philosophy is to describe language and not to interfere with the actual use of language.

Philosophy is a map of the terrain, but the map is not the terrain itself, just as a map of Arizona is not Arizona. Philosophy does not give us new information about language; it adds clarity by describing the language. We must assemble, select, and arrange. Only then do we have everything we need to solve the problem.

> We must do away with all *explanation*, and description alone must take its place. And this description gets its light, that is to say its purpose—from the philosophical problems. These are, of course, not empirical problems; they are solved, rather, by looking into the workings of our language, and that in such a way as to make us realize these workings: *in despite of* an urge to misunderstand them. The problems are solved, not by giving new information, but by arranging what we have always known. Philosophy is a battle against the bewitchment of our intelligence by means of language. [38]

LINKS TO PHENOMENOLOGY

The analytic philosophers wanted to limit philosophy to an analysis of language. They were also well aware of the relation between the world of everyday experiences and the physical world, but they thought they could solve this puzzle by a rigorous logical analysis of language. Phenomenologists disagreed with such limited views of language and took a different philosophical direction. Whereas analytic philosophers focused their work on clearing up language muddles and fuzzy thinking as in metaphysics, the phenomenologists actually encouraged complex and abstract language.

6

PHENOMENOLOGY
Husserl and Heidegger

I cannot live, experience, think, value and act
in any world which is not in some sense in me,
and derives its meaning and truth from me.
—Edmund Husserl

THE HUMAN EXPERIENCE

The analytic approach to philosophy dominated much of twentieth-century thought in the United States and Great Britain. Within continental Europe, however, especially Germany and France, interest in analytic philosophy waned. Two new philosophies caught the Europeans' attention, however: phenomenology and existentialism. Phenomenology set aside questions about objective scientific facts and recommended instead that we look within our subjective human experience for answers. The two most prominent philosophers of this new movement were Edmund Husserl and Martin Heidegger.

The word *phenomenology* comes from the Greek word *phainomenon*, meaning "how things appear." The use of the word *phenomenon* or *phenomenology* actually began earlier when Immanuel Kant used the word *phenomenon* (the world of our sense experience, such as taste, sight, sound) as opposed to *noumenal* (the world beyond our sense experience, such as God and immortality). Later, Georg Wilhelm Hegel used the word *phenomenology* in his account of the phenomenology of the mind. The phenomenologists agreed with Kant that human experience is limited to phenomena, but they disagreed that the things we experience are constructed by the mind.

In general, phenomenologists thought that the analytic philosophers made a big mistake by not including consciousness in their philosophy. The analytic philosophers believed we could only test facts because that is all we could understand. They had said that we could not test consciousness, so any talk about it was meaningless. Yet, the phenomenologists set out to show, like Alfred North Whitehead, that consciousness is important because all things in life experience it. "All consciousness is consciousness of something." Now, it was up to philosophy to describe how consciousness works.

EDMUND HUSSERL

Edmund Husserl, the modern founder of phenomenology, wanted to know how consciousness shapes reality and how the world "reveals itself" to consciousness. Rather than doubting everything as Descartes had, Husserl set to one side, or "bracketed," as he said, all his beliefs about something in order to look at it afresh. He wanted to step back from himself to observe consciousness working.

Husserl found that consciousness "sees" a unity in things. For example, when he looked at one side of a box, his mind still anticipated the entire box. Husserl's goal was to make philosophy a "rigorous science." He conducted his philosophy along the lines of a scientific experiment. He took the abstract notion of time, and by bracketing calendars, clocks, and the like, he found that he experienced time as eternal "now," in a flow from the past to the future. His experience would be similar to hearing a single note but knowing it is part of a song. Everybody, he said, experiences time in the same way.

Husserl's Life

Edmund Husserl (1859–1938) was born into a Jewish family in the town of Prossnitz, Moravia, which is now part of the Czech Republic. After his early education, he attended the University of Leipzig in Germany. Two years later, he transferred to Friedrich-Wilhelm University (named after Nietzsche) in Berlin to study mathematics and philosophy. In 1881, he enrolled in the University of Vienna where he received his Ph.D. in mathematics. While there, he attended the lectures of Franz Brentano, who, through his lectures on philosophers David Hume and John Stuart Mill, inspired Husserl to make philosophy his vocation.

Husserl briefly taught at the University of Halle in Germany, where he published his first book and married Malvine Steinscheider. They had three children and remained at Halle until 1901. In that year, he accepted a teaching position at the University of Göttingen that lasted for the next 16 years. There, he published many of his important philosophical works and developed his concept of phenomenology.

In 1916, the University of Freiburg in Germany offered him a full professorship. He accepted and taught there until he retired. While at Freiburg , he continued to work on various projects, including the manuscripts that would be published after his death. For the rest of his life, he remained in Freiburg, but the Nazis barred him from participating in any public academic activities during the last five years of his life because he was a Jew. The University of Southern California in the United States offered him a professorship, but he chose to stay in Freiburg, where he died at age 79.

Edmund Husserl, the Father of Phenomenology, believed that only by bracketing would philosophy become its own unique and rigorous science. He desired to shift the focus of philosophy away from broad theorization toward a more precise study of ideas and simple events.

The Crisis of Western Science

According to Husserl, Western science is in a crisis caused by the lack of belief in the rational mind. Over the years, he said, science has developed a wrong attitude about the world. The natural sciences view nature as physical and totally ignore the realm of spirit—knowing, valuing, and judging—because spirit cannot be studied objectively as a fact. Thus, by separating matter, which is objective, and spirit, which is subjective, Western science had made the world dualistic.

> With this the interpretation of the world immediately takes on a predominately dualistic, i.e., psychological form. The same causality—only split in two—embraces the one world; the sense of rational explanation is everywhere the same, but in such a way that all explanation of the spirit, in the only way in which it can be universal, involves the physical. There can be no pure, self-contained search for an explanation of the spiritual, no purely inner-oriented psychology or theory of spirit beginning with the ego in psychical self-experience and extending to the other psyche. The way that must be traveled is the external one, the path of physics and chemistry. . . . This objectivism or this psychophysical interpretation of the world, despite its seeming self-evidence, is a naïve one-sidedness. . . . To speak of the spirit as annex to bodies and having its supposedly spatiotemporal being within nature is an absurdity.[39]

According to Husserl, saying that science is simply physical is a mistake. So, we need to return to the Greek philosophers and study their view of the world. The Greeks lived a life of true philosophy, which is the "science of the world as a whole, of the universal unity of all being." This was the glorious foundation of Western philosophy, which through the ages had been lost, in Husserl's opinion. For Socrates, Plato, and Aristotle, the most important aspect of a person was the soul, rational and nonrational—a whole unit.

Husserl also criticized psychology for trying to be totally "objective" like physics.

> By its objectivism psychology simply cannot make a study of the soul in its properly essential sense, which is to say, the ego that acts and is acted upon. . . . More and more perceptible becomes the overall need for a reform of modern psychology in its entirety. As yet, however, it is not understood that psychology through its objectivism . . . simply fails to get at the proper essence of spirit; that in isolating the soul and making it an object of thought . . . it is being absurd.[40]

Bracketing

Phenomenology, said Husserl, is a descriptive analysis of subjective processes, or consciousness, based on intuition. Philosophy should describe the information received from consciousness without any bias. By intuitively studying the phenomena within our consciousness and reporting our findings, we are describing only what is given to consciousness. Such a study, he said, would put an end to speculation or guesswork.

Husserl's philosophy begins at what he called the "natural standpoint," the everyday world as experienced by each person. His method was to perform a "phenomenological reduction" of that experience. This involves ignoring all previously held personal, philosophical, and even scientific beliefs about something and then examining what remains. His aim was to show exactly how the mind works.

The method Husserl used was bracketing. By bracketing, he wanted to show how consciousness shapes reality. Rather than doubting everything, he bracketed all his beliefs about something and then looked at it anew. He found that consciousness "sees" a unity in things.

By bracketing his experience of things, that is, making no judgments about what exists or does not exist, he could look at his experiences without judging whether anything more than what he sees exists or does not exist. By bracketing, judgment meant that Husserl could observe consciousness at work.

The question arises: If we can bracket subject and object by setting them aside, is there anything left? Husserl would answer, "Yes, we have consciousness." It is a "pure" consciousness not tainted by prejudgments because consciousness is neither subjective nor objective, but a meeting of subject and object.

> Let us suppose that we are looking with pleasure in a garden at a blossoming apple-tree, at the fresh young green of the lawn, and so forth. . . . From the natural standpoint the apple-tree is something that exists in the transcendent reality of space, and the perception as well as the pleasure a psychical state which we enjoy as real human beings. Between . . . the real man on the one hand and the real apple-tree on the other, there subsist real relations. . . . Let us now pass over to the phenomenological standpoint. The transcendent world enters its "bracket"; in respect of its real being we use the disconnecting *epoche*. . . . Together with the whole physical and psychical world the real subsistence of the objective relation between perception and perceived is suspended; and yet a relation between perception and perceived (as likewise between the pleasure and that which pleases) is obviously left over, a relation which in its essential nature comes before us in "pure immanence." [41]

Husserl argued that when we suspend judgment by bracketing we become wholly detached. When we are wholly detached, we can observe the essential nature of pure consciousness. He called this pure consciousness the "transcendental ego."

Like Bergson, Husserl thought that intuition is the faculty of knowing. Intuition, he said, is a direct insight and the "source of authority for knowledge." We cannot doubt the truth of an intuition because it is totally nonjudgmental. Through this method, we can discover our true self. Husserl discovered that he was pure ego, with pure existence. Through the ego alone, the world and the beings in the world made sense to him.

By bracketing experience, we are led to the center of reality, the conscious self.

The Phenomenological Ego

For Husserl, the phenomenological ego is a philosophizing ego, a pure ego. The world is nothing more than the ego's awareness of it. It can be said, "As an ego, I am the stream of consciousness in which the world gets its meaning and reality." Husserl called the pure ego "the wonder of wonders," and he considered it a mystery that the world had a being (we humans) that could be aware of its own existence. According to Husserl, it is through the phenomenological ego that all truth can be found. While everything else is bracketed, the phenomenological ego is always present in experience. Consciousness makes up the world because it makes the world exist for *me*.

Because the world is made up of our own consciousness, we cannot know the world when we try to reach it through objective science. The world cannot be understood objectively. To understand the world, we must use phenomenology that holds scientific facts bracketed and allows us to view the world intuitively and see its reality.

Husserl's method of phenomenology influenced many philosophers in phenomenology and existentialism. Martin

Heidegger is among those who developed his philosophy on this new way of looking at the world.

MARTIN HEIDEGGER

Husserl wanted to understand how the world "reveals itself" to consciousness. Martin Heidegger's major interest was existence, or being, based on the fundamental philosophical question, "Why is there something rather than nothing?" Heidegger used Husserl's phenomenological method to determine an answer, but he did not bracket the outside world from individual consciousness. For Heidegger, we cannot separate ourselves from the world. We are "beings-in-the-world," he said.

Heidegger's Life

Martin Heidegger (1889–1976) was born in Germany's Black Forest region, where his father was custodian of the local Catholic church. As a young student, Heidegger's main interest was in the ancient Greeks and the classics. After elementary school, he attended a Jesuit school that gave him a solid education in the classics and Greek culture and language. Here, Heidegger was introduced to Aristotle's idea of being, and he became fascinated with the whole idea of being and its meaning. He was so intrigued with the subject that the study of "Being" became his life's work. Among his favorite philosophers were the ancient Greek pre-Socratics, Søren Kierkegaard, and Friedrich Nietzsche.

At the University of Freiburg, Germany, Heidegger began his studies in theology to become a priest. Two years later, under the influence of Husserl, he changed his major field to philosophy. After receiving his doctorate degree, he was Husserl's assistant until he was appointed as an associate professor at the University of Marburg, Germany. Through his association with Husserl, Heidegger became deeply interested in phenomenology and wrote his major work, *Being and Time*. After Husserl's retirement, Heidegger was appointed his successor to the chair of philosophy at the University of Freiburg. He dedicated his book to Husserl, but later when he departed from Husserl's method, he removed the dedication.

In 1933, the Nazis came to power and ousted the director of the University of Freiburg. Because Heidegger was a member of the Nazi party, he was chosen as the new director. A year later, he lost interest in the Nazi party, resigned as director, yet kept teaching until the end of the war. Because of his association with the Nazis, the French occupying forces banned him from teaching for five years following the war. In 1951, one year before his retirement, he returned to teaching.

Heidegger visited Greece and France before settling into a secluded life in a hut in the Black Forest, where he continued to write great philosophical works. Heidegger died at age 86. His collected works, *Gesamtausgabe,* was begun during his lifetime. Publication has not yet been completed, but when it is, it will comprise 100 volumes.

Heidegger's writing is notorious for its level of difficulty. Heidegger invented words, gave old terms new meaning, and put words together in such a way that translators disagree on their meaning. One word might be translated in several ways. Heidegger soared beyond the barriers of language, much to the alarm of analytic philosophers.

Heidegger wanted to help us clarify our understanding of our own being and of "Being" itself. By using the phenomenological method, he thought we should examine the human being to gain some understanding of "Being."

The Human Being, or *Dasein*

We start off with one of Heidegger's unique words: *Dasein,* which in German means "Being there." Humans, said Heidegger, should not be defined as objects. To be human, means to wonder about the relation between being and "Being." According to Heidegger, Dasein is the only being that shows concern for its own "Being." Dasein is aware of the present moment and its existence within us, the past, and what it could become in the future. Thus, Dasein's way of being involves having an understanding of its own Being. To designate the way of "Being" that characterizes Dasein, Heidegger chose the term "existence." Dasein *exists*.

> Dasein always understands itself in terms of its existence—in terms of a possibility of itself: to be itself or not itself. Dasein has either chosen these possibilities itself, or got itself into them, or grown up in them already. Only the particular Dasein decides its existence, whether it does so by taking hold or by neglecting. The question of existence never gets straightened out except through existing itself.[42]

Existence

Our uniqueness as human beings is in our existence because we can choose different kinds of being for ourselves. We are not as limited as beings that are not Dasein such as fish. Fish can never ask, "Why am I a fish and not a frog?" Unlike other creatures, we are uniquely free to develop our existence. "I am Dasein," said Heidegger. *I am* belongs to any existing human being and it is what makes us authentic or not. Authentic individuals are true to themselves and willing to take responsibility. Inauthentic individuals are not true to themselves, nor do they take responsibility. They live as society expects them to live: "But these are both ways in which Dasein's Being takes on a definite character, and they must be seen and understood *a priori* as grounded upon that state of Being which we have called '*Being-in-the-world*.'"[43]

Martin Heidegger is often regarded as one of the most original and important philosophers of the twentieth century. His main concern was the study of being, emphasizing language as the tool with which the question of being could be examined.

Being-in-the-World

Disagreeing with Descartes, who held that the human mind is a thinking substance and the body is a physical substance, Heidegger said the human being is not a thinking substance, and the world is not a physical substance. He said that Descartes's thinking portrays the world as if it were a container with human beings inside. Separating humans and the world is a false view, according to Heidegger.

Our basic state of human existence is our being-in-the-world. To be in the world as Dasein is not the same as one thing being in another thing, such as a fish in an aquarium or a jacket in the closet. We humans are not in the world as separate objects, but as "Being familiar with." To say, for example, that "she is *in* love" does not refer to her location, but to her type of being. To say, then, that we humans are in the world not only places us in space but describes the structure of our existence, which makes it possible for us to think meaningfully about the world.

Concern

Dasein means we are concerned with others, involved in projects, or using tools. For Heidegger, Dasein dwells in the world and is not simply located there.

> Being-in-the-world has always dispersed itself or even split itself up into definite ways of Being-in. The multiplicity of these is indicated by the following examples: having to do with something, producing something, attending to something and looking after it, making use of something, giving something up and letting it go, undertaking, accomplishing, evincing, interrogating, considering, discussing, determining. . . . All these ways of Being-in have *concern* as their kind of Being.[44]

Without human beings, there could be no world. We and our world are united. According to Heidegger, we have some sort of understanding of our own Being, and we do not understand our Being as a separate self. To find out what sort of understanding it is, Heidegger has us think of a clearing in the middle of a dark forest. The space within the clearing is one in which flowers and trees could appear. The clearing, he said, is Dasein: "[As] Being-in-the-world it is cleared in itself, not through any other entity, but in such a way that it is itself the clearing. . . . Dasein brings its 'there' along with it. If it lacks its 'there', it is not factically the entity which is essentially Dasein; indeed, it is not this entity at all *Dasein is its disclosedness.*" [45]

What is the "Being-there" that Dasein brings with it? Heidegger describes the "Being-there" of Dasein under three headings: (1) attunement, or mood; (2) understanding; and (3) discourse, or speech.

Moods

Dasein always finds itself in some sort of mood. Our moods disclose how we are coping with our existence. Moods color everything—joy, sadness, dread, pleasure, anger, and so on.

According to Heidegger, we are "thrown" into the world into circumstances beyond our control, such as our body type, our parents, the time and place we were born, and our race. Because of this, the world is not a place we can truly feel at home. We are, he said, orphans and homeless. Being thrown into the world means that we experience anxiety. Among moods, anxiety is the most unique because it has no object. Unlike fear or anger, a person suffering from anxiety cannot identify a specific cause of his or her anxiety.

Moods usually tell us something about ourselves, and anxiety is the mood that reveals the "Being" of Dasein as thrown into the world. Anxiety can motivate us to take responsibility for our actions and become our true authentic self. Anxiety can also motivate us to follow the crowd in an inauthentic way, such as Kierkegaard's "the crowd is untruth," and Nietzsche's herd mentality.

Understanding

Every mood we have brings some understanding of the world. For Heidegger, understanding is the root of our existence because we must have some understanding of "Being." Understanding, he said, is always confronted with "possibility." At this moment, you have a certain understanding of your possibilities: the possibility that you will watch television tonight, or meet a friend, or study. Understanding is part of our Being, and it is a part of our existence. "Dasein always has understood itself and always will understand itself in terms of possibilities," said Heidegger. Possibility is more basic to our Being than even the facts about us because these possibilities are inside us.

Now we can see how Heidegger differed from the analytic philosophers in his interpretation of understanding. The analytic philosophers said that we arrive at understanding when we have analyzed some whole into its simple parts. We can only understand the parts. Heidegger, however, believed that only when we understand the whole could we understand the parts.

Discourse

Discourse, said Heidegger, is an example of our mood and our understanding. Because all of us talk, discourse involves Being-*with*. Yet, discourse is not only talking. Discourse also can be silence, like that between good friends. For example, if two friends are sitting together and not speaking, the silence between them is a language that may speak more clearly than words. In their mood, they have reached an understanding. Sound, then, does not create the essence of language, and silence is not merely a gap in talking. We are, said Heidegger, only capable of "authentic" speech because we are capable of silence. If we are not rooted in silence, our talk becomes idle chatter or an attempt to impose our opinions on others, making us inauthentic. Speech is a characteristic of Dasein. The way we humans use speech makes it either authentic or inauthentic.

Heidegger asked, "What moves us from the inauthentic life to the authentic life?" His surprising answer was, "Our understanding that we are going to die." Our knowledge of death helps us understand our Being "fully as a whole."

Death

Although death is as commonplace as life, we seldom think of it as a part of ourselves. We know that other people, pets, and flowers die, but we do not come to grips with the fact that *I* am going to die. Death, said Heidegger, makes Dasein a *whole.* We have anxiety about death, but such anxiety should not be confused with fear. If we are to live an authentic life, we must think about death and not turn our minds from it.

> Anxiety in the face of death is anxiety "in the face of" that potentiality-or-Being which is one's ownmost, non-relational, and which is not to be outstripped. That in the face of which one has anxiety is Being-in-the-world itself. That about which one has this anxiety is simply Dasein's potentiality-for-Being. Anxiety in the face of death must not be confused with fear in the face of one's demise. This anxiety is not an accidental or random mood of "weakness" in some individual; but, as a basic state-of-mind of Dasein, it amounts to the disclosedness of the fact that Dasein exists as thrown Being *towards* its end. [46]

Although coming face-to-face with the possibility of death is terrifying, we must keep the threat of death constantly before us. Taking death into ourselves frees us from living an inauthentic life. Confronting death frees us to be ourselves as a whole.

LINKS TO THE EXISTENTIALISTS

Just as Husserl inspired Heidegger to use the phenomenological method, Heidegger was the source of many ideas for existentialist philosopher Jean-Paul Sartre. As Heidegger took phenomenology in a direction uncharted by Husserl, Sartre reversed Heidegger's position. Whereas Heidegger had wanted to find a means for understanding Being as a whole, Sartre concentrated on "existence" of the individual in a world without God. By concentrating on our existence, and not our essence, Sartre laid the foundation for a new philosophy called existentialism.

7

EXISTENTIALISM
Sartre, de Beauvoir, and Camus

Man is nothing else but what he makes of himself.
Such is the first principle of existentialism.
—Jean-Paul Sartre

THE BIRTH OF EXISTENTIALISM

Existentialism began in Paris, France, following World War II. The horrors of war triggered contemporary existential reactions in philosophy, art, and literature. The world was shocked by the death of roughly 72 million people, including millions of Jews in Nazi concentration camps, and the first use of atomic weapons. Jean-Paul Sartre, Simone de Beauvoir, and Albert Camus wrote of the horrors of the Holocaust, lived through the German occupation of France, and were involved with the French anti-Nazi resistance movement. All of them were profoundly affected by their wartime experiences.

Existential thinking came to life in French cafés among playwrights, novelists, poets, musicians, artists, and philosophers. These men and women met to discuss world affairs and the effects of historical events on people's lives. War, in particular, had a devastating effect on the feelings and aspirations of individuals. Technology, which arose as an aid to humankind, soon gathered a momentum of its own, forcing people to fit their lives into the rhythm of machines. Because of technology, because of war, because of the failure of religion, people were losing their markedly human qualities. People were becoming objects instead of subjects, being converted from an *I* into an *It.* Existentialists felt that, when we see each other as objects instead of subjects, we are in danger of a mechanistic view of humanity. Such a view brings with it anxiety, alienation, and fear. This group of intellectuals wanted to change the outlook to view people as real individuals.

Existential philosophers have no particular system because systems become mechanical. Existential opinions vary on religion and politics. These philosophers can be religious, agnostic, or atheists. Some are liberal, others moderate or conservative. Although many of their viewpoints differ, all existentialists agree on the importance of (1) the meaning of the individual, (2) freedom, (3) living an authentic life, (4) alienation, and (5) mortality.

Opposed to the scientific approach to human nature, existentialists turn their attention to the inner life of an individual. "Who am I?" "What does my life mean?" "Why do I feel guilty?" "Why am I afraid?" "What should I do to become the person I want to be?" These personal questions are shared by all individuals, and there is no objective, scientific answer to them.

Existentialists believe that we create our essence through our freedom of choice and moral responsibility. As human beings, we have the freedom to decide how we want to live. Kierkegaard, Nietzsche, Husserl, and Heidegger showed deep insight into the causes of human anxiety and conflict. Yet, philosophy for the most part dealt with the technical problems of metaphysics, ethics, and knowledge in a general and objective manner, leaving people's concerns about their personal destiny in the dust. Existential philosophers attempted to address these concerns, and, as they did, existentialism snowballed into one of the major philosophies of the twentieth century.

JEAN-PAUL SARTRE

Jean-Paul Sartre's name has become identified with existentialism for his formulation of the basic principle of existentialism: *Existence precedes essence.* This means that we create our essence through freedom of will and moral responsibility. This statement is a direct reversal of traditional metaphysics, which ever since Plato's time has said that, "Essence precedes existence," meaning our true self, or soul, is immortal and not created by us.

The philosophies of Karl Marx, Husserl, and Heidegger strongly shaped Sartre's thought. Sartre shared many of the political aims of Marx's communism, especially its goal of overthrowing capitalism. Yet, Sartre emphasized the individual whereas Marx emphasized the group. Sartre admired Husserl's phenomenological method, but he came to different conclusions about the human situation. He admired Heidegger, who was concerned with Being, but Sartre's concern was with Existence. Heidegger had said the only important moral issue is how we face the knowledge that we are going to die. For Sartre, an atheist, the only issue is our human situation in a world without God.

Sartre's message was simple: We are born into an existence that has no divine purpose. Life is often absurd or horrible, and the only true values are the ones we create for ourselves. He saw the world abounding with love and horror. People, he said, are capable of both courage in friendship and appalling cruelties to each other. Through random luck, some people are born to misery and early death, and some people are born into wealth, intellect, and health.

Sartre agreed with Marx and psychoanalyst Sigmund Freud that belief in God is childish. Over the centuries, millions of people have killed each other for their religious beliefs. The universe is indifferent to us. There is no right and wrong. If millions are killed in a war, the Sun continues to shine on both the killers and the killed. Nature does not care. We are born into a world that has no god dictating the rules. We are utterly alone in choosing how to live. According to Sartre, "Man is condemned to be free."

We have everything here on Earth that we need to make life good, and it is up to us to make it work. This is the obligation of an existentialist.

Sartre's Life

Jean-Paul Sartre (1905–1980) was born in Paris, an only child. His father was a naval officer who died when Sartre was a baby. His mother, part of a scholarly family and a niece of the great doctor/humanitarian/musician Albert Schweitzer, raised Jean-Paul in the home of her father, a professor at the University of Paris, also known as the Sorbonne.

Of himself, Sartre said, "I was small and homely, with eyes that could not focus." He had no playmates, so he stayed in their sixth-floor apartment and "sank into the world of books and ideas." Sartre knew he would be a writer because when he wrote he was most aware of existing. "By writing," he said, "I was existing. . . . I existed only in order to write."

An outstanding student, in the 1920s, Sartre was chosen for the esteemed École Normale Superiéure, one of France's most prestigious schools of higher learning. There, he became the leader of a circle of intellectual students who met in his room. Among them was Simone de Beauvoir. She and Sartre became lovers and settled into a partnership that lasted throughout their lives. To de Beauvoir's distress, however, Sartre occasionally had other lovers. Both Sartre and de Beauvoir were committed to their literary work, and both became famous writers. Before

Sartre would allow his manuscripts published, he insisted that she critique them.

After graduation in 1929, Sartre taught in schools in Le Havre, Laon, and finally, Paris. There, he published his first novel, *Nausea*. When the war broke out in 1939, he was drafted into the army and spent a year in a German prison camp. Upon being freed in 1941, he resumed teaching and writing, and later joined the French Resistance.

In 1951, he joined a Marxist group, but refused to join the French communist party because he was horrified by Soviet atrocities occurring in Europe. In 1964, he was awarded the Nobel Prize in Literature but rejected it—the only person ever to do so. He said the award represented the bourgeois trappings of success he had long opposed. "A writer must refuse to allow himself to be transformed into an institution," he told the Nobel Prize committee.

In the 1970s, his weak eyesight failed entirely, his health deteriorated, and he lost the ability to write. The French, however, did not forget their literary hero. When Sartre died in 1980, 50,000 people followed his coffin through the Paris streets.

The Human Situation

The most important human situation, said Sartre, is living in a world without God. What is such a world and what are we supposed to do in such a world? Without God, we have no eternal nature, no soul, and no essence to fall back on. Without God, it is useless to search for a universal meaning of life. Without God, we must decide for ourselves how to live. Without God, we cannot count on anyone but ourselves. We are alone, abandoned on Earth, without help, and with no goal except the one we set for ourselves.

In his novel *Nausea*, Sartre's main character, Roquentin, discovers that life is chaos. There is no reason to exist, yet we do

Jean-Paul Sartre was a philosopher, screenwriter, novelist, critic, and a founder of the existential school of philosophy. Sartre believed that people are free and conscious that they are free. Therefore, people are responsible for their own emotions and their own behavior.

exist, and we exist in an absurd and meaningless world. In such a world, we feel alienated, and that alienation creates a sense of despair, boredom, nausea, and absurdity. Yet, we must have such experiences before we can act.

In Sartre's play *The Flies*, Orestes says, "Human life begins on the other side of despair." Facing the fact that no God exists, humans feel abandoned. Because God does not exist, we cannot have faith in God as the center of our life. We must make our own center. Since there is no God, we cannot look for salvation in heaven.

Sartre insisted that, besides our existence, there is nothingness. There is no Plato's immortal soul, no Descartes's "I think therefore I am," and no Kierkegaard's subjective self. There is only nothingness, which "lies coiled in the heart of being, like a worm." In nothingness lies consciousness. We exist in consciousness. It is up to each of us to create our essence.

Creating our Essence

For Sartre, there is no God. Therefore, there cannot be a soul or inner essence. There is no human nature common to all humans and no essence that tells us what it means to be human. Thus, we feel abandoned in the world. Once in the world, however, we must act, and through our choices and actions, we become who we now are and who we will be in the future. The future is in our hands.

Sartre also believed that, when we choose something for ourselves, we are choosing for all other people. For instance, if you choose to join the Democratic Party rather than the Republican Party, you are saying that the Democratic Party is best for everyone. If you want to marry and have children, you are saying marriage and parenthood is best for all humanity, not just you alone. By the choices you make, you are creating a certain image of humanity.

> If . . . existence precedes essence, and if we grant that we
> exist and fashion our image at one and the same time, the
> image is valid for everybody and for our whole age. Thus
> our responsibility is much greater than we might have
> supposed, because it involves all mankind. If I . . . choose
> to join a Christian trade-union rather than be a communist, and if by being a member I want to show that the

best thing for man is resignation . . . I am not only involving my own case—I want to be resigned for everyone. . . .
If I want to marry, to have children, even if this marriage
depends solely on my own circumstances or passion or
wish, I am involving all humanity in monogamy and not
merely myself. . . . I am creating a certain image of man of
my own choosing. In choosing myself, I choose man. [47]

Consciousness

Because there is no God, there is no plan and no reason that
things happen as they do. Actually there is no reason for us to
exist at all. Still, our existence is different than that of a rock
or an insect. Existence does not simply mean that we are alive.
Plants and animals are alive, but they do not think about what
it means to be alive. We humans are conscious of our existence,
and that is why the being in humans is not the same being that
is in plants and animals. Humans are self-aware.

Consciousness means that we are conscious of something.
We are conscious of objects and conscious of our self. With
self-consciousness, we create who we are now and who we will
be in the future. We try our best to attain rocklike stability,
but we are doomed to the insecurity of our own being. Unlike
stones and insects, we can move beyond our given situation,
and this is not only our anguish, said Sartre, but our power
and glory as well.

Responsibility

In his categorical imperative, philosopher Immanuel Kant
asked, "Would I will [choose] that my actions become universal law?" In other words, if I am about to tell a lie, would I will
that lying become a universal law. Sartre said, "In choosing
myself, I choose man." This statement sounds a lot like Kant's
categorical imperative, but Sartre did not agree with Kant that

some actions, such as telling the truth, are always right and that other actions, such as breaking promises, are always wrong. When I make a certain choice, Kant would say, "in creating my own image, I am creating a value for all humankind." For Sartre, there is no universal law to guide our choices.

> The existentialists say at once that man is anguish. What that means is this: the man who involves himself and who realizes that he is not only the person he chooses to be, but also a law-maker who is, at the same time, choosing all mankind as well as himself, cannot help escape the feeling of total and deep responsibility. Of course, there are many people who are not anxious, but we claim that they are hiding their anxiety, that they are fleeing from it. Certainly, many people believe that when they do something, they themselves are the only ones involved, and when someone says to them, "What if everyone acted that way?" they shrug their shoulders and answer, "Everyone doesn't act that way." But really, one should always ask himself, "What would happen if everybody looked at things that way?" There is no escaping this disturbing thought except by a kind of double dealing. A man who lies and makes excuses for himself by saying "not everybody does that," is someone with an uneasy conscience, because the act of lying implies that a universal value is conferred upon the lie. [48]

Sometimes we would not want others to act as we do. For Sartre, however, it is self-deception or "bad faith" to say that it is all right for me to act that way because others *will not* choose to act that way. When we realize we are responsible for others as well as for ourselves, we face not a universal law, but a deep sense of anguish. Each choice we make is helping to create our world, and if we deceive ourselves by avoiding responsibility, our conscience will always bother us.

When we make excuses, we are being pessimistic, because excuses allow us to blame our genes, our environment, and our bad luck. We blame our parents or family situation for the way we turned out. For Sartre, such thinking is for cowards. The real hero knows we are fully responsible for what we are.

> What people would like is that a coward or a hero be born that way. . . .
>
> That's what people really want to think. If you've been cowardly, you may set your mind perfectly at rest; there's nothing you can do about it; you'll be cowardly all your life, whatever you may do. If you're born a hero, you may set your mind just as much at rest; you'll be a hero all your life; you'll drink like a hero and eat like a hero. What the existentialist says is that the coward makes himself cowardly, that the hero makes himself heroic. There's always a possibility for the coward not to be cowardly any more and for the hero to stop being heroic. What counts is total involvement; some one particular action or set of circumstances is not total involvement. [49]

Bad Faith

For Sartre, bad faith is trying to run away from the pain of freedom and responsibility. It is the way of cowards. Bad faith is present in most of our activities because we often try to hide a truth from ourselves. Bad faith is this self-deception; lying to our self about our motives. Sartre's example of bad faith is a woman who agrees to go out with a man whom she knows would like to have sex with her.

She knows also that it will be necessary sooner or later for her to make a decision. But she does not want to realize the urgency: she concerns herself only with what is respectful and discreet in the attitude of her companion. She does not apprehend this conduct as an attempt to achieve what we call "the first approach." [50]

During the date, the woman interprets whatever her companion says as having no sexual suggestion. When he takes her hand, she even separates herself from it by ignoring that her hand is in his. The woman, said Sartre, is not only deceiving herself about her companion, she is deceiving herself about her own desires. She is pretending that she is not a sexual being and that her companion's advances have nothing to do with her sexually. She is in bad faith for denying her own choice in the situation and for denying the situation itself.

In Sartre's example, the woman knows the truth but refuses to admit it to herself. Lying to herself is self-deception. Bad faith is not a conscious act but a "willful refusal to recognize our freedom," according to Sartre. Although bad faith is an ever-present threat, by being aware of this threat, we can overcome it.

SIMONE DE BEAUVOIR

Although Simone de Beauvoir never had children of her own, she is known as the Mother of Feminism. Her treatise *The Second Sex* (1949) was the first attempt to explore why women allowed themselves to be dominated by men. She wrote that all people should be free from gender prejudices. The work was so controversial that the Roman Catholic Church put it (along with her novel *The Mandarins*) on the Index of Forbidden Books. At that time, there was little serious philosophy on women from a feminist point of view. *The Second Sex* started the feminist revolution and remains to this day an important text in philosophy, feminism, and women's studies.

De Beauvoir is one of the most brilliant and esteemed French existentialist philosophers and writers to date. At age 21, she was the youngest student ever to pass France's difficult agrégation examination in philosophy. In 1954, *The Mandarins* received the esteemed Prix Goncourt Award, France's most prestigious literary honor.

De Beauvoir's Life

Simone de Beauvoir (1908–1986) was the elder of two daughters born into an upper-class French family, which eventually lost their money. When the servants were let go, the domestic chores fell on Simone's mother, Françoise, who resented her lot but never questioned that housework was a woman's duty. Françoise was a devout Catholic, and as a young girl, Simone enjoyed attending church. She studied in a Catholic school and considered God her personal companion. At age 14, however, she lost her faith and decided there was no God. Although her loss of faith left her very lonely, she remained an atheist until her death.

Since the age of nine, de Beauvoir knew she wanted to be a writer. When she lost her faith, she expected writing to take the place of God. She later admitted, however, that she had expected too much, but still she wrote. While a student, Simone discovered philosophy and met Jean-Paul Sartre, among other young intellectuals. Some of these men and women formed a group they called "the Family." The Family consisted of writers, actors, and activists who got together for intellectual stimulation and socializing for more than 60 years.

From the day they met, de Beauvoir and Sartre formed a relationship that lasted all of their lives. They were both brilliant writers and both achieved fame for their literary works. In fact, de Beauvoir was considered first among women of letters.

At the time of Sartre's death, she was France's most celebrated living writer. Her relationship with Sartre, however, was not always happy. Sartre had an affair with another woman, Olga. Of their situation, de Beauvoir said, "From now on we will be a trio instead of a couple." Sartre always said that de Beauvoir was his "privileged" but not his only female companion. His philosophy was "one can always be free." But de Beauvoir asked, "What is the freedom of the women in a harem?" She decided to have a relationship with an American writer, but when he asked her to marry him, she said she would not put anyone before Sartre.

De Beauvior was terrified of growing old because society, in her eyes, treated old people just as it treated women—as second-class citizens. After Sartre died, she published a farewell to him that included details of the last 10 years of Sartre's life and revealed his many illnesses, including his blindness. In the conclusion she wrote, "My death will not bring us together again. This is how things are." After Sartre's death, she continued writing, traveling, and being involved in political work. In 1981, de Beauvoir died of a respiratory illness. She was 78.

The Second Sex

In her work *The Second Sex*, de Beauvoir wrote that women were oppressed. From the beginning, she said, man has seen himself as *self* and woman as *other*—not as man's equal. The other is a threat to self, and men think that, if they are to be free, they must subordinate women to themselves. Men take a superior role by exploiting women's biological functions and look upon women as "a womb, an ovary." The male's sperm leaves his body so that "the male recovers his individuality intact." Yet, the fertilized egg implants in the uterus. "First violated, the female is then alienated, she becomes, in part, another than herself." Thus, it is harder for a woman to become

Simone de Beauvoir produced a vast body of writings on ethics, politics, fiction, autobiography, and feminism. She strongly believed customs and laws needed to be changed in order that women be treated as equal to men. De Beauvoir was an ardent women's rights activist in the 1970s, participating in demonstrations, as well as writing and speaking on many women's issues.

an independent self, especially if she has a child. Woman is looked upon as body.

> The enslavement of the female to the species and the limitations of her various powers are extremely important facts; the body of woman is one of the essential elements in her situation in the world. But that body is not enough to define her as woman; there is no true living

reality except as manifested by the conscious individual through activities and in the bosom of a society. Biology is not enough to give an answer to the question that is before us: why is woman the *Other?* [51]

De Beauvoir insisted that woman is more than a mere body. Like Sartre, she said we create ourselves. There is no such thing as a basic female nature or a basic male nature. She resented the views of women given by psychoanalysts Alfred Adler and Sigmund Freud. Freud based women's inferior and subservient social status on a castration complex. Because women lack the organ that symbolizes superiority and authority, they suffer what Freud calls "penis envy." Total nonsense, said de Beauvoir. Women do not want a penis. Instead, they want the privileges that society bestows upon those with a penis. De Beauvoir's "penis prestige" means power. Women are considered the *other* not because they lack penises but because they lack power.

> When a little girl climbs trees it is, according to Adler, just to show her equality with boys; it does not occur to him [Adler] that she likes to climb trees. For the mother her child is something quite other than an "equivalent of the penis." To paint, to write, to engage in politics— these are not merely "sublimations"; here we have aims that are willed for their own sakes. To deny it is to falsify all human history. [52]

Myths About Women

According to de Beauvoir, as civilization developed, men controlled women by creating myths about them. In these myths, woman fulfills what man lacks, and she is as changeable as a chameleon. The myths urge the ideal woman to deny herself. De Beauvoir gave five examples of such myths:

1. Woman exists to make her man feel masculine.
2. Woman gives up being what she wants to be so her man can be what he wants to be.
3. Woman is the handmaid not only to God but also to man.
4. Woman carries the burden of guilt; if her love is strong enough, she can make or break her man.
5. Woman risks life and limb to save her lover from ruin, prison, or death.

According to de Beauvoir, if women could simply laugh at all of the above, the situation would be less dangerous. Unfortunately, the most horrible part of the way man defined woman was that many women believed it. Women, de Beauvoir said, have been programmed to see themselves through men's eyes.

Becoming a Woman

One of de Beauvoir's most frequently quoted statements is, "One is not born, but rather becomes a woman." From their earliest years, girls are told their bodies are different, and both family and society teach girls that they are here to marry and have children. Their roles of wife and mother limit women's freedom. Even if a woman chooses a career, she must always be and act like a woman. As a result, she develops an inner conflict between her professional and her feminine interests.

If a woman wants to change her role and put an end to the limits imposed upon her, de Beauvoir suggested three strategies she could use:

1. Go to work. Share in the job experience.
2. Become intellectual. Study, think, and participate in intellectual matters.

3. Work toward changing society into one that no longer judges men and women as self-other, subject-object.

Above all, said de Beauvoir, women must help themselves change the self-other outlook. Using Sartre's notion of bad faith, she said some women have bad faith about their own humanity. They treat themselves as sexual objects to deny their freedom. If both men and women could see each other as equals, then it "would bring about an inner metamorphosis [change]."

> The fact that we are human beings is infinitely more important than all the peculiarities that distinguish human beings from one another; it is never the given that confers superiorities: "virtue," as the ancients called it, is defined at the level of "that which depends on us." In both sexes is played out the same drama of the flesh and the spirit, of finitude and transcendence; both are gnawed away by time and laid in wait for by death, they have the same essential need for one another; and they can gain from their liberty the same glory. If they were to taste it, they would no longer be tempted to dispute fallacious privileges, and fraternity between them could then come into existence. [53]

ALBERT CAMUS

Although Albert Camus refused to call himself an existentialist, he definitely represents the existential movement. Existentialism characterizes the human situation in the world as a revolt against the "absurd," and one of Camus's main themes is, "Life is absurd." According to Camus, the important thing is not to know whether life is worth living but *how* we must live it, with all the suffering it entails.

Camus's Life

Albert Camus (1913–1960) was born in Algeria, Africa, to a poor working-class family. When Albert was only one year old, his father died in battle during World War I. His mother was deaf and illiterate, and suffered a serious speech impediment. She worked as a housemaid to support the family. Albert shared a small apartment in a poor district in Algiers with his mother, his brother, a grandmother who was dying of cancer, and a paralyzed uncle. The apartment was dark, and cockroaches climbed the stairs. Of these living conditions, Camus later wrote:

> I think of a child living in a poor district. That neighborhood, that house! There were only two floors, and the stairs were unlit. Even now, long years later, he could go back there on the darkest night. He knows that he could climb the stairs without stumbling once. His very body is impregnated with this house. His legs retain the exact height of the steps; his hand; the instinctive, never-conquered horror of the banister. Because of the cockroaches. [54]

Alluding to his childhood poverty, Camus said, "It is in this life of poverty, among these vain or humble people, that I have most certainly touched what I feel is the true meaning of life." He felt deep love for his mother and remembered her as a silent, uncomplaining, and kind woman who never stopped working. Her character influenced him throughout his life.

In school, one of his teachers, Louis Germain, recognized Camus's intelligence and helped him get a scholarship to one of the better high schools that would make it easier for him to attend college. Camus greatly appreciated Germain's efforts, and when Camus won the Nobel Prize in Literature in 1957, he dedicated it to his former teacher.

His high school teacher Jean Grenier introduced Camus to the writings of Plato, Kierkegaard, and Nietzsche. During high school, Camus was active in sports, especially soccer, but his involvement with sports abruptly ended at age 17 when he contracted tuberculosis. The physical and emotional effects of tuberculosis, including bouts of depression, would plague Camus the rest of his life. Camus left his family's crowded, unhealthy apartment and moved in with his wealthier uncle, who provided him with clothes, books, and the example of a cultured social life.

At age 19, Camus attended the University of Algiers, where he worked odd jobs and began studying philosophy. While at the university, Camus joined the Communist Party but became discouraged with it and soon left. He was active in drama presentations, writing, acting in, and directing plays. While working on his doctoral studies, his tuberculosis recurred and during the next five years, he spent much of his time in a sanatorium. His bright outlook and love of nature took a dark turn. He became bitter, protesting the cruelties of life and developing an obsession with the absurd. Unfortunately, his health kept him from completing his doctorate and acquiring a teaching certificate.

At the beginning of World War II in 1939, Camus went to Paris to sign up with the military, but because of his health, the army refused him. Instead, he edited an underground newspaper for the French Resistance. The suffering, waste, and death of the war disturbed him deeply. He asked, "If life is absurd, is there any reason not to commit suicide?" For Camus, this question has to arise when a person stops deceiving himself and begins to see the world as it is.

The next year, after a short-lived marriage to Simone Hie, he married Francine Faure, a pianist and mathematician. While editing a Resistance newspaper in 1942, he wrote two of his most popular works, *The Stranger* and *The Myth of Sisyphus*. The popularity of these books made Camus an international celebrity.

When Camus won the Nobel Prize in 1957, he was the second-youngest writer ever to receive the prize. With the prize money, he bought a house in the Alps where he could write in privacy. For the first time in his life, Camus was financially independent.

Camus was only 46 when he died in an automobile accident. A rear tire of his car blew out, and the car struck a tree. Camus died instantly. Ironically, he had once said that he could not imagine a death more meaningless than dying in a car accident.

The Absurd

According to Camus, anyone who does not live in denial must view life in this world as absurd. The absurd means we live with anxiety and stress. We are born innocent, prepared to love and to live happily. We want a good world, but the world is not good—it is insane. We want justice and honesty, but the world is unjust and dishonest. We look for reason, but the world is not rational. We have dreams of a good life, but the world does not care about our dreams. Absurdity means there is no "ultimate reason" why things are as they are. Simply put, it is a "bad fit" between humans and the world: "In a universe suddenly divested of illusions and lights, man feels an alien, a stranger. His exile is without remedy since he is deprived of the memory of a lost home or the hope of a promised land. This divorce between man and his life, the actor and his setting, is properly the feeling of absurdity." [55]

Only when we face the fact that we are strangers in a strange land and the world is absurd can we face how to live our lives and how to die. Camus is famous for his question, "If life is absurd, should we commit suicide?" Answering his own question,

Albert Camus was a philosopher, journalist, playwright, and novelist who addressed many issues facing humanity, including political violence, suicide, the death penalty, and terrorism. He believed that the absurdity of human existence could only be made less harsh through moral integrity.

Camus, an atheist, said, "Even if one does not believe in God, suicide is not legitimate." Recognizing the absurd, he said, is an "invitation to live and create in the very midst of the desert."

Revolt

Revolt, said Camus, can be a very good thing, because it is a method to help us discover meaning in our existence. Revolt affirms the absurd and thus gives us the courage to live without kidding ourselves and without committing suicide. Revolt means abandoning traditional worldviews that define the world, God, and humans. Revolt also means refusing to cooperate with any society that tries to impose its dishonesty on us and with a world that would crush our dreams to pieces.

> The revolt gives life its value. Spread out over the whole length of a life, it restores its majesty to that life. To a man devoid of blinders, there is no finer sight than that of the intelligence at grips with a reality that transcends it. The sight of human pride is unequaled. . . . [To] impoverish that reality whose inhumanity constitutes man's majesty is tantamount to impoverishing him himself. I understand then why the doctrines that explain everything to me also debilitate me at the same time. They relieve me of the weight of my own life, and yet I must carry it alone. [56]

Through revolt, said Camus, we find our freedom and our innocence. By revolting against the absurd, we become free to do whatever we want because we know there is not any future or any being superior to us. There are no absolute moral laws. Through revolt against the absurd, anything is permitted because all is equally right and wrong. We become our own masters without guilt. We regain our innocence. We are free. Camus did not believe we should revolt by following our blind passions. He would not support robbery or other criminal acts. Revolt, he said, is rational and moral, but we must not think our revolting will improve the world. An absurd world offers no guarantees.

The Myth of Sisyphus

Camus introduced his philosophy of the absurd in a 1942 essay entitled *The Myth of Sisyphus.* Sisyphus was a character from ancient Greek mythology who is condemned to push a huge rock up a mountain to the top. Every time he gets the rock to the top, however, it rolls down the mountain to the bottom. Undaunted, Sisyphus walks down the mountain, gets behind the rock, and pushes it up again. The task that that could never be completed would last forever.

In the ancient myth, Sisyphus asked the god Pluto permission to return to Earth from Hades to punish his wife. Permission granted, he comes to Earth. Yet, Sisyphus becomes so happy on Earth that he refuses to return to the underworld. The gods threaten him, but to no avail. Zeus then sends the god Mercury to snatch Sisyphus from Earth and take him forcibly to Tartarus, the lowest and most horrendous level of Hades "where his rock was ready for him."

In *The Myth of Sisyphus,* Camus writes, "The gods had condemned Sisyphus to rolling ceaselessly a rock to the top of a mountain, whence the stone would fall back of its own weight. They had thought with some reason that there is no more dreadful punishment than futile and hopeless labor." [57]

> You have already grasped that Sisyphus is the absurd hero. He *is* as much through his passions as through his torture. His scorn of the gods, his hatred of death, and his passion for life won him that unspeakable penalty in which the whole being is exerted toward accomplishing nothing. This is the price that must be paid for the passions of this earth. . . .
>
> It is during that return, that pause, that Sisyphus interests me. A face that toils so close to stones is already stone itself! I see that man going back down with

a heavy yet measured step toward the torment of which he will never know the end. That hour like a breathing-space which returns as surely as his suffering, that is the hour of consciousness. At each of those moments when he leaves the heights and gradually sinks toward the lairs of the gods, he is superior to his fate. He is stronger than his rock.

If this myth is tragic, that is because its hero is conscious. . . .

The struggle itself toward the heights is enough to fill a man's heart. One must imagine Sisyphus happy. [58]

As the hero of the absurd, Sisyphus is aware that he can never rest, nor can he escape the futility of his task or even die. Sisyphus is Camus's example of revolting against the absurd in life. "The struggle itself toward the heights is enough to fill a man's heart. One must imagine Sisyphus happy." The role of Sisyphus is exactly how Camus saw the human condition: the will to revolt against the absurd as the way to create value for life.

LINKS TO THE FUTURE OF PHILOSOPHY

In our complicated world, we struggle with technical questions such as curing AIDS, finding solutions to critical environmental problems, terrorism, cloning, stem-cell research, crime rates, drug abuse, and so on. These questions involve current issues that are important to a particular time and place. They are what philosophers call "timely questions," and we try to solve these timely questions with factual information such as alternative gas fuels, cancer-fighting drugs, and improving national security. Timely questions are important, but they address situations that are only part of the human condition. Seldom, if ever, do timely questions suggest that we examine our lives.

Socrates said, "The unexamined life is not worth living." The twenty-first century is the age of Socrates once again. The answer to timely questions should depend on our insight into the enduring questions, to what Plato and Aristotle called the philosophical sense of wonder. Who am I? How should I live? What happens when I die? Are people basically good or bad? Is it better to be good than evil? Does might make right? Is there a God? How did the universe come to be? What will make me happy?

The journey to know yourself and to understand your relationship with the world and the divinity might well be our reason to be. The task is not easy, but as the great Jewish philosopher Benedict de Spinoza wisely said, "All noble things are as difficult as they are rare." The future of philosophy is bright—it is in your hands.

NOTES

CHAPTER 1

1. Jeremy Bentham. *An Introduction to the Principles of Morals and Legislation*, Ch. 1, Sec. 1. London: Oxford University Press, 1823.
2. Ibid., Ch. 111, Sec. 9.
3. John Stuart Mill, *Autobiography*. Edited by J.D. Stillinger. London: Oxford University Press, 1971, pp. 83–84.
4. Ibid., pp. 97–98.
5. John Stuart Mill, "What Utilitarianism Is," Ch. 2, in *Utilitarianism*. Chicago: University of Chicago Press. XXX, pp. 448–449.
6. Ibid., p. 453.
7. Ibid., p. 451.
8. Ibid., pp. 272–273.

CHAPTER 2

9. *The Journals of Kierkegaard*, translated and edited by Alexander Dru. London: Collins, 1958, p. 44.
10. Ibid., p. 4.
11. *Kierkegaard's Concluding Unscientific Postscript*, translated by D.F. Swenson, notes and introduction by W. Lowrie. Princeton, NJ: Princeton University Press, 1941, p. 276.
12. *Either/Or*, translated by Howard V. Hong and Edna H. Hong, Vol. 1. Princeton, NJ: Princeton University Press, 1983, pp. 285–286.
13. Friedrich Nietzsche, *The Gay Science*, translated by Walter Kaufmann, Book 5, Sec. 344. New York: Vintage Books, 1974, p. 283.
14. Ibid., Book 5, Sec. 343, p. 280.

15. Friedrich Nietzsche, *Thus Spake Zarathustra*, translated by Walter Kaufmann, in *The Portable Nietzsche*, Part 1. New York: Vintage Books, 1974, pp. 126–127.
16. *The Gay Science*, op. cit., Sec. 341, p. 273.

CHAPTER 3

17. William James, *Pragmatism*, edited by Ralph Barton Perry. Cleveland: World Publishing, 1964, pp. 126–127.
18. William James, *The Meaning of Truth*, edited by Ralph Barton Perry. Cleveland: World Publishing, 1964, p. 224.
19. William James, "The Moral Philosopher and the Moral Life," in *The Moral Philosophy of William James*, edited by John K. Roth. New York: Thomas Y. Crowell, 1969, pp. 180–181.
20. William James, *The Varieties of Religious Experience*. New York: Longmans, Green, 1962, pp. 516–517.
21. William James, *The Search for Meaning in Life*, edited by Robert F. Davidson. New York: Holt, Rinehart and Winston, 1962, p. 61.
22. John Dewey, *How We Think*. Boston: Heath, 1937, pp. 100–103.
23. John Dewey, *Human Nature and Conduct*. New York; Henry Holt, 1922, pp. 98–99.

CHAPTER 4

24. Henri Bergson, *An Introduction to Metaphysics*, translated

by T.E. Hulme, 15th ed. Indianapolis: Bobbs-Merrill, 1978, pp. 21–22.

25. Henri Bergson, *Creative Evolution*, translated by Arthur Mitchell. New York: Random House, 1944, p. 72.

26. Henri Bergson, *Two Sources of Morality and Religion*, translated by R. Ashley Auden and Cloudesley Brereton. New York: Henry Holt, 1935, pp. 27–28.

27. Ibid., p. 317.

28. Alfred North Whitehead, *Modes of Thought*. New York: Macmillan, 1925, p. 27.

29. Alfred North Whitehead, *Science and the Modern World*. New York: Macmillan, 1925, p. 29.

30. Ibid., p. 137.

31. Ibid., pp. 250–257.

CHAPTER 5

32. Bertrand Russell, "Logical Atomism," in *Logic and Knowledge*. London: George Allen & Unwin, 1956, p. 197.

33. Bertrand Russell, *Religion and Science*. London: Thornton Butterworth, 1935, pp. 230–231, 235–236.

34. Bertrand Russell, *Marriage and Morals*. New York: Liveright, 1929, pp. 291, 293.

35. Bertrand Russell, *Principles of Social Reconstruction*. London: Allen & Unwin, 1916, p. 163.

36. Ludwig Wittgenstein, *Tractatus Logico-Philosophicus*, translated by D.F. Pears and B.F. McGuinness. London: Routledge and Kegan, 1961, p. 3.

37. Ludwig Wittgenstein, *Philosophical Investigations*, translated by G.E.M. Ancombe, Sec. 11–15. New York: Macmillan, 1953.

38. Ibid., Sec. 109.

CHAPTER 6

39. Edmund Husserl, "Philosophy and the Crisis of European Man," translated by Q. Lauer, in *Phenomenology and the Crisis of Philosophy*. New York: Harper & Row, 1965, pp. 184–185.

40. Ibid., pp. 187–188.

41. Edmund Husserl, *Ideas: General Introduction to Pure Phenomenology*, translated by W.R. Boyce Gibson, Sec. 88. New York: Macmillan, 1931.

42. Martin Heidegger, *Being and Time*, translated by J. Macquarie and E. Robinson. New York: Harper & Row, 1962, p. 61.

43. Ibid., p. 78.

44. Ibid., p. 83.

45. Ibid., p. 171.

46. Ibid., p. 295.

CHAPTER 7

47. Jean-Paul Sartre, *Troubled Sleep*, translated by G. Hopkins. New York: Bantam Books, 1960, pp. 280–287.

48. Jean-Paul Sartre, *Existentialism is a Humanism*, translated by Bernard Frechtman, 1957, in *The Fabric of Existentialism: Philosophical and Literary Sources*, edited by Richard Gill and Ernest Sherman. Englewood Cliffs, NJ: Prentice-Hall, 1973, p. 522.

49. Ibid., p. 527.

50. Jean-Paul Sartre, *Being and Nothingness*, translated by H.E. Barnes. New York: Philosophical Library, 1956, p. 66.

51. Simone de Beauvoir, *The Second Sex*, translated by H. M. Parshley. New York: Vintage Books, 1989, pp. 36–37.

52. Ibid., p. 51.

53. Ibid., p. 728.
54. Albert Camus, "The Wrong Side and the Right Side," in *Lyrical and Critical Essays,* translated by Ellen Kennedy, edited By Philip Thody. New York: Alfred Knopf, 1968, p. 26.
55. Albert Camus, *An Absurd Reasoning,* in *The Myth of Sisyphus & Other Essays,* translated by Justin O'Brien. New York: Vintage Books, 1955, p. 5.
56. Ibid., pp. 40–41.
57. Albert Camus, *The Myth of Sisyphus,* in *The Myth of Sisyphus & Other Essays,* op. cit., p. 89.
58. Ibid., pp. 89–91.

GLOSSARY

absurd   Lacking any rational explanation or orderly relationship.

altruism   The capacity to promote the welfare of others.

analytic philosophy   The view that the object of philosophy is to clarify the meaning of language by logical analysis.

atheist   One who believes there is no God.

bad faith   For Sartre, bad faith is self-deception by trying to run away from responsibility.

bracketing   Husserl's term meaning to set aside all beliefs about something and to look at it anew.

calculus of felicity   In Bentham's view, calculating the action that would produce the greatest amount of pleasure.

closed morality   For Bergson, a morality for the good of the group but one that excludes those outside the group.

Dasein   For Heidegger, *Dasein* means that human beings exist in the world; "Being-in-the-world."

determinism   The belief that everything that happens must happen exactly the way it does and that human beings have no free will.

dialectic process   A question-and-answer technique used by Socrates that leads one from mere opinion to knowledge.

dynamic religion   For Bergson, a religion in which individuals are unconcerned with dogma.

élan vital   For Bergson, the force that directs evolution.

empirical   Originating in or based on observation or experience.

essence   For Sartre, through our choices and actions we create the person we are now and who we become in the future.

essential self   For Kierkegaard, our true relationship with God.

evolution   A process of gradual, progressive change and development.

existentialism   The philosophy that focuses on the individual person, usually stressing choice, freedom, and the problem of existence.

feminism   The view that women and men should be treated as equals.

free will   The view that human beings have free and independent choice that is not determined by divine or physical forces.

hedonism   The pursuit of pleasure; any philosophy that views pleasure as good and pain as bad.

herd mentality   A view in Nietzsche's philosophy that ordinary people are followers and do not think for themselves.

Index of Forbidden Books   A list of publications that the Catholic Church censored for being a danger to itself and to the faith of its members.

instrumentalism   For Dewey, the method to create a better society by reorganizing our social environment, especially education, through experimentation.

intuition   Direct and clear insight into basic truths.

logic   The laws of thought or reason; thinking correctly.

logical atomism   For Russell, a logically perfect language.

logical positivism   The philosophy of the Vienna Circle whose members viewed statements as meaningful only if verifiable by direct observation.

master morality   For Nietzsche, the morality of natural leaders with noble souls.

metaphysics   The branch of philosophy concerned with explaining the ultimate nature of reality, being, and the world.

mystic   One who experiences an intimate union of the soul with God; one who understands the secret mysteries of the universe.

natural selection   For Darwin, the processes in nature by which forms of life best able to adapt to environmental changes survive.

objective   An impartial, nonpersonal view.

open morality   In Bergson's view, the open morality is for the good of all human beings.

paradox   A seemingly contradictory or absurd statement that expresses a possible truth.

phenomenological ego   For Husserl, the stream of consciousness in which the world gets its meaning and reality.

phenomenology   Husserl's method of analysis that studies the structures of consciousness and of things as they appear to consciousness.

philology   The study of literary texts and of written records to establish their authenticity and meaning.

pragmatism   From the Greek word *pragma* meaning "action"; pragmatism's test for truth is what works best for us.

principle of utility   For Bentham, that which produces pleasure, good, or happiness for the individual and for the community.

process philosophy   The view that everything in the universe is interrelated and in process.

slave morality   In Nietzsche's view, slave morality consists of natural followers, the weak and powerless; herd mentality.

static religion   For Bergson, a religion with structured rules: dogma, ritual, doctrine.

subjective   Concerning the person, the individual.

superman   For Nietzsche, the ideal person.

utilitarianism The view that an action is good or right if it produces the greatest happiness or pleasure for the greatest number of people.

verification Demonstrating something to be true by logical rules.

verification principle Anything that cannot be proved, such as, "Metaphysical statements can be rejected."

Vienna Circle A group of scientists and philosophers at the University of Vienna who wanted to develop a new logic to prove that our knowledge is limited to sense experience; logical positivists.

will to power According to Nietzsche, the one thing all people have in common.

BIBLIOGRAPHY

Bentham, Jeremy. *An Introduction to the Principles of Morals and Legislation.* London: Oxford University Press, 1823.

Bergson, Henri. *Creative Evolution.* Translated by Arthur Mitchell. New York: Random House, 1944.

———. *An Introduction to Metaphysics.* Translated by T.E. Hulme. Indianapolis: Bobbs-Merrill, 1978.

———. *Two Sources of Morality and Religion.* Translated by R. Ashley Auden and Cloudesley Brereton. New York: Henry Holt, 1935.

Camus, Albert. *An Absurd Reasoning,* in *The Myth of Sisyphus & Other Essays.* Translated by Justin O'Brien. New York: Vintage Books, 1955.

———. *The Myth of Sisyphus & Other Essays.* Translated by Justin O'Brien. New York: Vintage Books, 1955.

———. "The Wrong Side and the Right Side," in *Lyrical and Critical Essays.* Translated by Ellen Kennedy. Edited by Philip Thody. New York: Alfred Knopf, 1968.

de Beauvoir, Simone. *The Second Sex.* Translated by H. M. Parshley. New York: Vintage Books, 1989.

Dewey, John. *How We Think.* Boston: Heath, 1937.

———. *Human Nature and Conduct.* New York: Henry Holt, 1922.

Either/Or. Translated by Howard V. Hong and Edna H. Hong. Princeton, NJ: Princeton University Press, 1983.

Heidegger, Martin. *Being and Time.* Translated by J. Macquarie and E. Robinson. New York: Harper & Row, 1962.

Husserl, Edmund. *Ideas: General Introduction to Pure Phenomenology.* Translated by W.R. Boyce Gibson. New York: Macmillan, 1931.

———. "Philosophy and the Crisis of European Man," in *Phenomenology and the Crisis of Philosophy.* Translated by Q. Lauer. New York: Harper & Row, 1965.

James, William. *The Meaning of Truth.* Edited by Ralph Barton Perry. Cleveland: World Publishing, 1964.

———. "The Moral Philosopher and the Moral Life," in *The Moral Philosophy of William James.* Edited by John K. Roth. New York: Thomas Y. Crowell, 1969.

———. *Pragmatism.* Edited by Ralph Barton Perry. Cleveland, OH: World Publishing, 1964.

———. *The Search for Meaning in Life.* Edited by Robert F. Davidson. New York: Holt, Rinehart and Winston, 1962.

———. *The Varieties of Religious Experience.* New York: Longmans, Green, 1962.

The Journals of Kierkegaard. Translated by Alexander Dru. London: Collins, 1958.

Kierkegaard's Concluding Unscientific Postscript. Translated by D.F. Swenson. Princeton, NJ: Princeton University Press, 1941.

Mill, John Stuart Mill. *Autobiography.* Edited by J.D. Stillinger. London: Oxford University Press, 1971.

———. "What Utilitarianism Is," in *Utilitarianism.* Chicago: University of Chicago Press. [Author: Date of publication?]

Nietzsche, Friedrich. *The Gay Science.* Translated by Walter Kaufmann. New York: Vintage Books, 1974.

———. *Thus Spake Zarathustra,* in *The Portable Nietzsche.* Translated by Walter Kaufmann. New York: Vintage Books, 1974.

Russell, Bertrand. "Logical Atomism," in *Logic and Knowledge.* London: George Allen & Unwin, 1956.

———. *Marriage and Morals.* New York: Liveright, 1929.

———. *Principles of Social Reconstruction.* London: Allen & Unwin, 1916.

———. *Religion and Science.* London: Thornton Butterworth, 1935.

Sartre, Jean-Paul. *Being and Nothingness.* Translated by H.E. Barnes. New York: Philosophical Library, 1956.

———. *Existentialism is a Humanism.* Translated by Bernard Frechtman, in *The Fabric of Existentialism: Philosophical and Literary Sources.* Edited by Richard Gill and Ernest Sherman. Englewood Cliffs, NJ: Prentice-Hall, 1973.

———. *Troubled Sleep.* Translated by G. Hopkins. New York: Bantam Books, 1960.

Whitehead, Alfred North. *Modes of Thought.* New York: Macmillan, 1925.

———. *Science and the Modern World.* New York: Macmillan, 1925.

Wittgenstein, Ludwig. *Philosophical Investigations.* Translated by G.E.M. Ancombe. New York: Macmillan, 1953.

———. *Tractatus Logico-Philosophicus.* Translated by D.F. Pears and B.F. Mc Guinness. London: Routledge and Kegan, 1961.

FURTHER READING

BOOKS

Bentham, Jeremy, and John Stuart Mill. *Classical Utilitarians: Bentham and Mill.* Translated by John Troyer. Indianapolis: Hackett Publishing, 2003.

Drake, David. *Sartre.* London: Haus Publishing, 2005.

James, William, and John Dewey. *James and Dewey on Belief and Experience.* Edited by John M. Capps. Champaign: University of Illinois Press, 2004.

Moran, Dermot, and Roger Luckhurst. *Edmund Husserl: Founder of Phenomenology.* Cambridge: Polity Press, 2005.

Nietzsche, Friedrich. *Portable Nietzsche.* Edited and translated by Walter Kaufmann. New York: Penguin Group, USA, 2003.

Richardson, William J. *Heidegger: Through Phenomenology to Thought.* Bronx, NY: Fordham University Press, 2002.

Russell, Bertrand Arthur. *The Problems of Philosophy.* New York: Oxford University Press, USA, 1997.

Solomon, Robert C. *Dark Feelings, Grim Thoughts: Experience and Reflection in Camus and Sartre.* New York: Oxford University Press, USA, 2006.

Stallknecht, Newton Phelps. *Studies in the Philosophy of Creation: With Especial Reference to Bergson and Whitehead.* Edited by Donald L. Jennermann, David A. White, and Marilyn C. Bisch. Lewiston, NY: Edwin Mellen, 2001.

Stroll, Avrum. *Wittgenstein.* Oxford: Oneworld Publications, 2007.

Tidd, Ursula. *Simone de Beauvoir.* Oxford: Taylor & Francis, 2003.

Turnbull, Neil. *Get a Grip on Philosophy.* New York: Time-Life Custom, 2003.

WEB SITES

http://plato.stanford.edu/entries/kierkegaard/

http://plato.stanford.edu/entries/nietzsche/

http://www.friesian.com/existent.htm

http://www.iep.utm.edu/a/analytic.htm

http://www.iep.utm.edu/p/processp.htm

www.iep.utm.edu/

www.phenomenologyonline.com/

www.philosophypages.com/hy/6q.htm

www.pragmatism.org/

www.utilitarianism.com/

PICTURE CREDITS

INDEX

ABOUT THE AUTHOR

JOAN A. PRICE has a Ph.D. in philosophy from Arizona State University. She was a philosophy professor at Mesa Community College for 30 years and cofounder of the Department of Religious Studies. She was chairperson of the Department of Philosophy and Religious Studies for five years and is presently professor emeritus of philosophy at Mesa Community College.

Joan has written dozens of magazine and journal articles and is the author of *Truth is a Bright Star: A Hopi Adventure*, translated into Japanese and Korean; *Hawk in the Wind; Medicine Man; J.K. Rowling: A Biography; Understanding Philosophy*; and *Great Religious Leaders* for middle-grade and young adult readers. Her adult books include *Introduction to Sri Aurobindo's Philosophy; Philosophy Through the Ages*, a textbook for college students; and *Climbing the Spiritual Ladder*.

She is an animal lover with three dogs and several flocks of wild geese and ducks that camp on the lake by her house for daily handouts. She lives in Scottsdale, Arizona.